Duart Castle in Lockdown

Ray Canham

Copyright © 2021 Ray Canham

Author photo by Alison Canham

All rights reserved.

ISBN: 9798528790145

DEDICATION

This book is dedicated to everyone who has visited
and supported Duart Castle, contributed time, money
and encouragement and to those who work tirelessly
around the world to help preserve Duart for future
generations.

CONTENTS

	Acknowledgments	i
	Introduction	1
	Glossary	6
1	How did I end up here?	8
2	Background	12
3	Meet the team	19
4	January	21
5	What's in a name?	28
6	Sir Lachlan Maclean	29
7	February	35
8	Torosay	41
9	Anne Clothier	43
10	March	50
11	Coat of Arms	56
12	Alasdair Barne	59
13	April	61
14	Parlour games	66
15	Alison Canham	68

16	May	72
17	Castles everywhere	81
18	Andrew Bradley	83
19	June	89
20	Going up and down	98
21	Fiona Steel	100
22	July	106
23	Location, location, location	112
24	Jonathan Schiavone	114
25	August	119
26	Royal connections	128
27	Carol Wagemakers	130
28	September	135
29	More film connections	144
30	Behzad Reza-zadeh	146
31	October	151
32	Black's Tower	157
33	Arianna Pretorius	159
34	November	161
35	Surveys	168

36	Andrew Maclean	170
37	December	173
38	How far?	182
39	Fallout	185
40	Virtue Mine Honour	193
41	What a Year That was	196
	About the Author	200

ACKNOWLEDGMENTS

This book would not be possible without the cooperation and support of many people. I'd be mortified if I missed anyone out so a general round of applause to everybody who has assisted, be that in practical help, words of encouragement, submitting their contributions or just being a splendid example of the human race and a pleasure to be around.

A specific thank-you to the cast and crew of Duart in lockdown 2020; Sir Lachlan Maclean, Anne, Arianna, Fiona, Carol, Andy, Bezhad, Jonny, Andrew Maclean and honourable mentions to Alasdair Barne and Neil Wilkinson.

To those who have gone before – Junelle, Stuart, Neil, Jean, Nic and all the ex-guides, tearoom and shop staff and 'Duart girls and boys' too numerous to mention.

To Martyn and Liz, for being there and understanding.

None of this would have been possible without the Chief, Sir Lachlan Maclean and all of the Macleans around the world who make Duart what it is.

Finally, to Alison because she's quite super.

Thank you.

Duart Castle in Lockdown

INTRODUCTION

The year 2020 was unusual for most of us. For many it was an undeniably tough time. When the Covid-19 pandemic hit, it did so with a ruthlessness that left trauma and loss in its wake. Families were torn apart, jobs were lost, mental health suffered, and lives were changed forever.

Around the world people perished and governments struggled while individuals faced the challenge head on. From health care workers to delivery drivers, shop workers to volunteers, people came together and carried on in the face of the virus as wave after wave of inspirational stories of individual and community action countered the bleak news bulletins.

This is a book about living through 2020 in extraordinary circumstances. Much of it was spent locked down at a 14th century castle on a remote peninsula of an island off the west coast of Scotland. The rest was devoted to operating a tourist attraction and business at the castle in challenging circumstances.

In many ways, we were lucky. We had a small but strong and stable team, glorious scenery around us and plenty of space in which to roam. We formed our own little bubble and developed routines and distractions to keep us going.

We lived, worked and played as a team against the backdrop of magnificent west coast landscape and the solid stone walls of Duart Castle, ancestral home of the Clan Maclean.

In this book we will be hearing from the people who were here, for some or all the year. Sir Lachlan Maclean - 28th Chief of the Clan Maclean, Anne Clothier - Retail Manager, Alison Canham – Personal Assistant to the Chief and Castle Guide, Fiona Steel - Tearoom Manager, Carol Wagemakers - Gardener, Andy Bradley - Stonemason, Behzad Reza-zadeh - Builder, Jonathan Schiavone - Carpenter, Arianna Pretorius - Relief Tearoom Manager, and Andrew Maclean - youngest son of the Chief and furloughed from his main employment. We will also hear from Alasdair Barne, a nephew of the Chief and Covid survivor.

This book is a stand-alone account of one tumultuous year that, for a host of reasons, will never be forgotten. It is not an authoritative account or an official Clan Maclean publication. It is very much my version of events. Interspersed through the book are personal stories from the people who lived and worked here during the 2020 season. Duart is a team and without everyone pulling together we would never have survived it.

It is light-hearted in nature. I am not trying to gloss over a serious subject like Covid-19, but a little light relief can be a good tonic. I am neither a politician or a scientist and therefore I have tried to stay clear of politics and science. Do not expect debates about masks, vaccines or government policy.

I decided to write it for two reasons.

Firstly, because of the reduced numbers of visitors I spent a good deal of 2020 on my own in the castle or the ticket hut. In such circumstances my mind wandered, and I took to writing ideas in my notebook. Some of these probably should not see the light of day ever again. For example; why don't geese inflate when they honk while flying? Would Vlad the Impaler have turned out differently if he were called Nigel?

Other ideas became the foundation for my book The Mitchley Waltz.[1] As I had written a fair chunk of it in 'work' time I felt I owed something in return.

Secondly, I wanted to contribute in some way to the castle restoration. I'll explain about that later on, but for now it is important to know that it relies upon visitors to fund around half the cost of the work. All profit from the various parts of the business goes towards the work. A year with drastically reduced visitor numbers hit us hard.

Very hard.

One afternoon in October, I sat on the castle steps feeling the last warming rays of the sun as it sunk below the mountains. The sky was golden and the only sound came from the ocean lapping at the shore. The last visitors were making their way to the car park. A child was skipping ahead lost in its own world

---

[1] Yes, that is a shameless plug.

of sunshine and holidays, making precious memories.

It was a perfect moment. I put my headphones on and prepared to go out and empty the bins. In my ears Nick Cave sung:

> *'Outside I sit on the stone steps,*
> *With nothing much to do*
> *Forlorn and exhausted,*
> *By the absence of you'*

Sitting alone on the stone steps, this melancholy refrain from the solo version of his song Brompton Oratory embraced me and sparked the idea for a book. Of course, I had another to finish first but one day I'd get around to it.

That day came when I handed my completed manuscript for The Mitchley Waltz over to Alison, my wife, for editing in January 2021 and I dared broach the subject with my boss and the owner of Duart Castle, Sir Lachlan Maclean, hereafter known as the Chief.

As you are reading this, I probably don't need to tell you that he said yes.

The first three chapters introduce some of the key subjects and characters, before we plunge on into my month-by-month account of the year. It is chronological, although occasionally I've taken small liberties when placing events into particular months to even out the diary chapters. Rest assured it all happened, broadly in the sequence that you read here. Perhaps I have occasionally exaggerated for comic effect – I will let you be the judge of that!

I take full responsibility for any errors, omissions

or awful jokes that may have crept in. I hope that you enjoy reading it as much as I have enjoyed reminiscing and writing about Duart in lockdown.

One final note of introduction before we continue.

All the proceeds of this book are going to the castle restoration appeal. The agreement I have is that for writing and collating it I get to promote my other books. I have borrowed the odd passage or two from them in the first two chapters, but otherwise you will be relieved to know that everything else is brand new.

GLOSSARY

The following may be of benefit.

Loch – Fresh water lake or sea water inlet or fjord. The term loch is used for both. For example, Loch Linnhe, which Duart overlooks, is a sea loch and Loch Ba on Mull is a freshwater loch.

Glen – Valley.

Burn – Stream.

Coo – Highland cow.

Keep – The central, most fortified building in a traditional castle. In the case of Duart the Great Tower is sometimes referred to as the keep.

First Minister for Scotland - The leader of the Scottish Parliament.

Level 0 – 4 – Graduated tiers of restrictions on movement, travel and business in Scotland.

NHS – National Health Service.

Hogmanay – New Year Eve to New Year Day in Scotland. Such is the usual party atmosphere that Scotland has two days of public holiday on the 1st and 2nd of January.

IrnBru – A Scottish carbonated soft drink with a flavour not unlike bubble gum.

Trews – Trousers.

Pants – Used here as the British names for underwear.

Holyrood – The seat of the Scottish Parliament.

Notes:

I have used English spellings, so if you are reading this in the USA or elsewhere you may find more 'U's' in words than you are used to and less 'Z's', pronounced 'Zed' over here by the way. Consider it a trade-off.

The castle is usually open from April to October. Therefore comparison figures for visitor numbers only include these months.

All figures quoted were correct at the time of writing in March 2021.

1 - HOW DID I END UP HERE

In my job as a castle guide one of the questions I frequently get asked is, *'you don't sound like a local...how did you end up here?'*

It's usually said in a curious tone and out of genuine interest. Occasionally it is uttered as if by a dignitary visiting a prison and quizzing a trustee. You can sense them thinking that greeting people in a cold castle in one of the UK's wettest spots is a form of cruel and unusual punishment.

It is a difficult question to answer. Not because I don't remember, although I have been known to check my name badge before signing my timesheet. It is because the answer is quite convoluted, and the castle isn't about me and my story. I try to keep it simple; a love of history and a job opportunity is the short answer. And I consider it a privilege, not a penance.

But as you are here, imagine that you have just wandered up a set of spiral stairs, you've passed the old pantry with the mannequin of a maid staring out of the window and walked down the corridor admiring the prints of Duart Castle from the 18th Century. Walking into the Sea Room with its panoramic views of sea and mountains, you approach the guide with his name badge on upside down and shirt tail hanging out and ask him…

'You don't sound like a local…how did you end up here?'

Alison and I were married in September 2015, after meeting at a friend's camping trip four years previously. Between us we have approximately three grown up children, a car, a motorhome and a lot of books and records. We share a passion for the great outdoors, hiking, camping, music and coffee.

We've both worked all our lives, Alison predominately in administration and me as a nurse for people who have a learning disability, and then in social housing in a series of jobs with increasingly long and bewildering titles.

Our prime years, the ones between wondering what to do with our lives and wondering where they went, could have continued in the same pattern, endlessly rebounding between home and work, getting stuck in traffic, trudging round the supermarket, paying the mortgage, saving for holidays and wishing our lives away.

Instead in 2016 we tested our six-month-old marriage by resigning from our jobs, selling our house, and spending eight months travelling around the United Kingdom living in a motorhome, who we christened Mavis, after the soul singer and civil rights activist Mavis Staples.

On our journey we worked at music festivals. We ended up playing kazoos with a biker gang, one of us appeared onstage with 80's pop legend Paul Young and we met Hope, the worst assistance dog in the universe, among many other adventures. We covered over 10,000 miles around the UK, and on the way, we fell in love with Scotland while searching for a place to call home.

Our adventures formed the backbone of my first book, Downwardly Mobile.

I'm not sure that we ever found somewhere we really felt was home until we washed up on the shores of the Isle of Mull. We had employment, a motorhome and…well that was pretty much it really.

We had committed to four months' work over the summer, to buy a little time to consider what to do next. But our growing fondness for the island and its people led us to extend our first season and then to return for a second.

At the end of that second season, we remained on Mull over the winter, temporarily moving into a cottage on the castle site. We had made new friends and started to really appreciate island life. Alison had become a member of the local church and I was writing and generally practising social distancing long before it became fashionable. We ambled along at a pace that allowed us to enjoy the views along the way, stop and chat to people we passed in the street and we learnt to make do and mend.

To borrow a phrase, 'getting downwardly mobile opens your eyes to really living.'[2]

Before our third stint at the castle for the 2019 season, we moved back into Mavis. The cottage was

---

[2] From the song The Reason, by Andy Flannagan

to be used as a home for seasonal staff and we cherished our privacy. Before long we were settled into familiar routines. We welcomed some of the regular Duart team back and some new recruits and we dived into another season of work.

Towards the end of 2019, we moved back into the cottage, this time permanently. Mavis was parked up outside, looking rather forlorn and unused except as an occasional temporary home for the builders working on the castle restoration.

During the winter of 2019 and early 2020 we both worked at the castle. Alison had become the Chiefs Personal Assistant, a job she split with looking after the online commerce for the giftshop. I became, in all but name, the caretaker. I looked after the building and grounds, painted, and generally spruced up the site ready for the torrent of visitors to come flooding in as soon as we opened the castle gates for the 2020 season…or so we thought.

2 - BACKGROUND

For the benefit of international readers (and possibly a few UK ones too) Scotland is a country in the United Kingdom. It makes up about one third of the total UK land mass and has a population of around 5.46 million people, whereas England has 56.29 million, although I have not counted them all so don't blame me if I'm a few out. Wales and Northern Island make up the rest of the UK.

Off the west coast of Scotland are a rather pleasing cluster of rugged islands called The Hebrides. They range in size from the 2,178 km^2 (841 mile^2) of Lewis and Harris, which are separate entities but comprise one landmass, to tiny lumps of rock that are home to a few seabirds and not much else. They are divided into the Inner and Outer Hebrides, denoting their proximity to mainland Scotland.

Mull is an inner Hebridean island of 875.35 km^2 (337.97 mile^2) with a coastline that looks like it has been drawn by a drunken cartographer during an earthquake. The terrain is agreeably corrugated, with some notable hills and mountains, picturesque lochs, green wooded glens, and some of the most stunning seascapes you could ever imagine.

It is home to approximately 3000 people, but that swells considerably during a normal tourist season. Tourism in one form or another is its primary economic activity, with farming, aquaculture, fishing, and a little forestry as well. The principal town is Tobermory, noted for its colourful houses and home of the children's television programme Balamory. Smaller settlements are scattered around the island, invariably hugging the coast and each distinct in character.

The island of Mull has some interdependent satellite isles. The most famous is Iona, which is separated from Mull by a narrow but lively stretch of the Atlantic and served by its own small ferry. Its best known for its Abbey and association with 1st Century Abbot and missionary St. Columba.

Other islands in Mulls orbit include Erraid, which is accessed at low tide by walking across the sand and was featured in the novel Kidnapped by Robert Louis Stevenson; Inch Kenneth, once home to socialite and National Socialist friend of Adolf Hitler Unity Mitford; Ulva, which was the birthplace of Lachlan Macquarie, who was Governor of New South Wales from 1809–21, and uninhabited Staffa, which is known for Fingal's Cave, which inspired the composer Felix Mendelssohn to write The Hebrides (Fingal's Cave) Overture in the 1830s.

Visitors have been coming to Mull for centuries. Some were welcomed, like the pilgrims travelling to Iona, and others, the Vikings of the 9th century for example, not quite so appreciated by the locals.

Today three ferries connect the island to the

mainland. One keeps Tobermory connected to Ardnamurchan, a remote peninsula which boasts a lighthouse at the most westerly point of mainland UK, and halfway down the west coast of Mull the Fishnish to Lochaline ferry chugs over the narrow Sound of Mull.

The main ferry route for most though is the 45-minute Oban to Craignure route, which in 2019 delivered over 652,000 passengers, nearly 170,000 cars, 7,000 commercial vehicles and close to 2,000 coaches to our shores[3]. Things would be quite different in 2020, as we shall see.

Once these vehicles clattered up the ramp of the ferry, along the pier and chose to turn right towards Tobermory or left towards Iona, they were faced with around 200km of roads. These mostly hug the coast and except for approximately 30 energetic kilometres, it is all single-track with passing spaces.

This adds an exciting unpredictability for the visiting motorist, from the scared witless through to the cautious and all the way to the downright reckless.

In Still Following Rainbows I wrote about how different people cope with passing spaces. Below is an abridged extract:

Locals
Two local drivers approaching one another will judge the passing space to perfection, requiring the person with the space to swerve lightly around the oncoming vehicle which may, in extreme circumstances require one or both parties to momentarily reduce speed to fewer than three digits.

---

[3] Figures from Calmac website.

Commercial vehicles and buses
Even locals find it best to tuck in and wait for the breeze and swaying to subside before venturing on. The driver will give you a half-hearted thanks by raising his hand while staring straight ahead.

Newcomers
You can always tell someone new to island driving. They are the ones sitting in passing spaces weeping. They spend their first day hopping from space to space, sometimes sending their children on ahead to scout out the road. They pull over as soon as they see another vehicle, even if it's on a different island.

Late for the ferry
They will just keep driving at you, irrespective of where the passing spaces are. We've been forced into narrow roadside gullies, soggy verges, and hedges by people rushing towards us like they are in the outside lane of the motorway.

To add to the motorists delight we have all manner of reckless wildlife to contend with, deer that seem to pop into existence when you least expect them, sheep that will run down the road for half a mile rather than step onto the safety of the lush grass verge, suicidal otters and cows that decide to feed their young in the middle of the highway.

If you were to approach a random stranger anywhere in the world and ask what Scotland meant to them, the chances are their answer will include: Haggis, The Loch Ness Monster, bagpipes, Outlander and clans.

The first four do not feature in this book, although someone tall and handsome from Outlander did visit the castle tearoom and giftshop a couple of years ago. I know this because there was a lot of squealing, frantic adjusting of hair and hastily touched up makeup from the ladies working in the tearoom at the time.

The clan though is central to the story of Duart as it is the home of the Chief of the Clan Maclean.

A clan is, in essence, a tribe or kinship with a shared identity through ancestral ties. They usually originated in specific geographic areas, although today people bearing a clan name may be spread around the world, as is the case for the Macleans.

The Macleans trace their lineage as a clan back to early 13th century Gilleain na Tuaighe, or Gillean of the Battle Axe, from the Kingdom of Dál Riata. Maclean's soon held land on Mull. The Macleans of Duart are first recorded in a papal dispensation of 1367.

There are many variations of the spelling of Maclean that have arisen over time. I have stuck here to the spelling used by the Chief, as one word with no capitalisation of the L. I'll cover other spellings later in the book.

The Macleans, like most influential clans of old, had allies of smaller clans. These were known as septs, families that followed another clan's Chief, or part of the extended clan family that hold a different surname. Some sources list over 160 septs for the Macleans, for example Rankin, Black, Beaton and MacBeth.

Travelling to Mull by ferry, passengers looking to the port side (that's left) will see the formidable Duart Castle standing on a cliff overlooking the Sound of Mull. It was probably the site of a dun or ring fort in earlier times and was fortified around the 12th Century as a castle of enclosure, essentially a stone wall with wooden buildings inside.

The castle as we know it today was built in the 14th Century by the 5th Chief of the Macleans, Lachlan Lùbanach (Lachlan the crafty). He married Mary Macdonald, daughter of the Lord of the Isles, and in doing so was granted the land that included the earlier fortification, where he built what we now know as Duart. The only easily recognisable part today from that era is the Great Tower.

Since those days the castle has witnessed its share of spirited and often bloody events, including inter-clan warfare and the marooning of a Chief's wife on a rock in the Sound of Mull (spoiler alert, she was rescued). It has played host to hostages from a Spanish Armada ship that subsequently blew up in Tobermory Bay, been attacked by Cromwellian warships, including three that sank off Duart Point, been seized by the English Crown and taken by 'fire and sword' by the Duke of Argyll's forces. The castle lay in ruins for over 160 years until Sir Fitzroy Maclean, 26th Chief bought it back for the clan in 1911 and set about turning it into his home.

The current Chief is the 28th and like all the previous Chiefs he is a descendant of Gillean. He is a Maclean from his bonnet to his toes and carries the name with pride. So much so that he is a full-time resident of the castle and has made it his ambition to complete the restoration and repairs to Duart, which are considerable and to which you have contributed by purchasing this book. Thank you.

Commencing in 2014, the first six phases of the restoration have been completed at a cost of £1.7 million. Phase six was completed between lockdowns in 2020 and early 2021. Work was carried out to the Keep wall and the roof above the Sea Room, the east courtyard wall and the steel beams the Banqueting Hall were replaced.

Phase seven comprises work to the wall facing the carpark, with an expected completion date of mid-2021. The final three phases are being planned now and the Appeal is currently seeking to raise over £200,000 to start phase eight later in 2021. If the target is not reached, then the scope of work will be reduced.

So, that's the castle, now let us meet some of the characters who will be accompanying us during our year in lockdown.

3 – MEET THE TEAM

We will be hearing peoples individual accounts elsewhere in this book, so for now we can content ourselves with a brief introduction.

Sir Lachlan Maclean Bt. of Duart & Morvern

28th Chief of the Clan Maclean. Retired, former soldier, businessman and the resident owner of Duart Castle.

Anne Clothier
Duart Shop Retail Manager.

Alison Canham
Personal Assistant to the Chief, Castle Guide.

Fiona Steel
Tearoom Manager.

Andrew (Andy) Bradley
Stonemason and lead contractor.

Jonathan Schiavone.
Director at The WoodKeeper Ltd, conservation of wooden artefacts and structures.

Behzad Reza-zadeh
Builder and general 'jack of all trades'.

Arianna Pretorius
Relief Tearoom Manager.

Carol Wagemakers
Castle Gardener.

Andrew Maclean
The Chief's youngest son.

Alasdair Barne
The Chief's nephew.

Neil Wilkinson
Neil has kindly supplied the weather data. He lives at Fishnish on Mull, which tends to be slightly colder, dryer and significantly less windy than Duart. The statistics given herein are to provide a flavour of the changing year. Temperatures are in Celsius.

Note: As two Andrews appear in our story, I refer to Andrew Bradley by his given 'site' name of Andy and Andrew Maclean as Andrew.

4 – JANUARY 2020

Towards the end of 2019 an outbreak of suspected pneumonia cases in Wuhan City, China is deemed serious enough for the authorities to alert the World Health Organisation (WHO). In January 2020 Human-to-human transmission of the new virus is confirmed. Cases are detected in Thailand, Japan, South Korea and the US as well as China.

On the island of Mull, the sun shone. Not for the whole of January you understand, but briefly and according to the weather forecast, in sufficient amounts for me to start one of the winter jobs I had been putting off. This involved taking out the wooden boards that line the driveway up to the castle, staining them, cutting back the turf they hold in check and then putting the freshly revamped boards back.

Simple.

Half an hour in, struggling to extract the second of 25 boards it rained. Of course it did.

Rain up here can be a curious phenomenon. For one thing you can usually see it coming. Often, we'll be bathed in sunshine watching a shower make its way down the Sound of Mull, the waterway that separates us from the mainland.

Once it reaches Duart what you think will be a passing downpour turns into a monsoon like torrent of horizontal water that attacks you from every angle. If it misses you, it'll bounce off the ground and fall again for a second go. Meanwhile the wind, rain's co-conspirator in the 'let us soak Raymond while he's working' precipitation fiesta, has developed the trick of being able to drive bullet like raindrops through 12 layers of protective clothing.

If this sounds like I take it personally, then that is because I do.

Ten minutes after stashing the two boards away I squelched inside, dripping and swearing in equal amounts.

'Hello dear,' Alison said in greeting, 'been for your morning swim?'

Fortunately, my response was muffled by the sweater I was clumsily trying to pull over my head. I feared it had shrunk in the deluge.

'I think we need a break,' Alison added, and went off to get scissors to release me from jumper bondage.

Two days and seven sweaters later I had got the rest of the boards out, so we pointed the car towards the Fishnish ferry for a jaunt over to the mainland. The plan was to drive from Lochaline, where the ferry docked, up through the glorious scenery of Morvern, a picturesque chunk of Scotland where it can be so peaceful you can hear a deer break wind in the next glen, then onto Fort William to stock up on essentials, like new underclothing. It is a fact of life on Mull that you can buy artisan chocolate, twenty different flavours of soap, local cheese in abundance, biscuits, cuddly lobsters and hiking boots, but nowhere sells underpants.

Morvern proved to be just as stunning as we predicted, radiant hills of auburn and russet, fast flowing burns and mist hugging the floor of the glens and seeping like smoke from woods of stately pines.

Snubbing the convenience of the Corran ferry and a short drive to the foundation garment paradise of Fort William, we continued along the increasingly narrow single-track road beside the banks of Loch Linnhe towards our first stop – the hamlet of Glenfinnan.

Glenfinnan is known for two things, the monument to clansmen who gave their lives to the Jacobite cause and the sweeping majesty of its 21 arch railway viaduct.

The monument stands at the head of Loch Shiel and was built in 1815 to mark the spot where, in August 1745 around 1,200 Highlanders gathered to pledge their allegiance to Prince Charles Edward Stuart and the start of the ill-fated 1745 Jacobite rebellion.

Due to the time constraints of relying on ferries and the lure of shopping we did not have time to climb the 18m (59ft) high monument, but we scrambled up a trail from the carpark to a viewing point where to our south we could appreciate the monument in its stunning setting and facing north we got to admire the viaduct.

Our vantage point meant we were able to get a clear view away from the hordes of other visitors, many from abroad, who flock here, even out of season. The viaduct is indeed a magnificent sight as it sweeps around 30m (100ft) above the glen below. But what brings people out in such numbers is its association with the fictional wizardry of Harry Potter. In the films the Hogwarts Express puffs across the viaduct on its way to Hogwarts.

The line is the Fort William to Mallaig section of the West Highland Line, opened in 1901 and often cited as one of the top railway journeys in the world. One sight that we didn't get to see was the steam engine, The Jacobite Express, passing over the viaduct. The train is still in service and regularly transports tourists along the line.

We took pictures, the obligatory selfie and took advantage of our National Trust for Scotland (NTS) membership by using the lavatories for free. I'm at the age where any journey longer than putting the bins out is planned around toilet stops and Alison liked the idea of getting value for money from her membership. Technically we had free parking as well but from what I could see no one else had bothered to buy a ticket and I'm sure they weren't all NTS members.

The gift shop was everything I expected and feared it would be. Expensive trinkets, jam labelled '𝔭𝔯𝔢𝔰𝔢𝔯𝔳𝔢' so that they can add an extra 20% on the price, biscuits that are more wrapping than confectionary and oodles of Harry Potter merchandise.

Still, we succumbed to something sweet and sticky to accompany our coffees which, with hindsight I like to think helped the NTS in a small way considering the decimation of the tourist season they were about to experience.

We pootled along to Fort William where we were

able to stock up with all the underclothing and food we could squeeze into our car, and then zipped down to Oban for our ferry home with the satisfaction of knowing we could face the forthcoming season with a full pantry and clean pants.

A couple of days later I was all alone at Duart. That morning I had deposited Alison and the Chief at the ferry terminal, kissed one of them goodbye and waved to the other, then watched them depart for the Glasgow Trade Fair. This annual orgy of consumerism is where we stock up on the goods for the gift shop and tearoom.

Anne had diligently dispatched her shopping list from New Zealand, where she was wintering, and Fiona and Arianna joined the shopping party at Glasgow. I escaped because someone had to mind the fort, literally.

My plan was to see them off, dive into the local shop as soon as the ferry pulled out and to be back home with a mountain of confectionary, fizzy pop and all the things I am usually forbidden, before their ferry reached Oban.

Armed with my stash I spent the next couple of days full of sugar, playing music at ear splitting volume and falling asleep on the sofa.

It was heavenly.

As was the return of my beloved. Alison that is, along with the Chief. I could not help noticing that both of them were burdened with considerably more luggage than they left with, as they staggered down the gangplank and up to the waiting car under the weight of several tote bags stuffed with booty.

Time was, back when I lived in the real world, I

had to attend conferences and trade events and I fondly recall the combination of stealth and subterfuge required to come away with a good haul of branded tat.

My hopes then were high. I expected at least enough free memory sticks to download the contents of the British Library. As soon as we arrived home, I could tell that Alison was a novice at this. She hadn't even packed a disguise so that she could go around looting the trade stalls for their free samples a second time. At least she had some free coffee, which was agreeable and counteracted my three-day sugar coma nicely.

With the Chief and Alison back home, the castle seemed to be getting busy. Anne had confirmed that she would be returning, Fiona would be joining us soon, Arianna was available to help out during the season and Andy was back at work. People were booked to move the scaffolding around; Jonny and Behzad were taking some of the castle windows out for repair and a team of stonemasons were busy doing butch things with power tools.

We had the core team here or on their way, the castle restoration was back in full swing, we had fresh pants and a full larder…what could possibly go wrong?

January 2020

Dry days 1,
Max temperature 11.6,
Min temperature 0.4,
Max wind speed 39.4 mph,
Monthly rainfall 14.17 mm.

5 – WHAT'S IN A NAME?

Duart comes from the Gaelic words Dubh Ard, which mean 'Black Point.' Fitting since the castle stands atop a bleak and rocky peninsular.

The name Maclean means 'Son of Gillean', after Gillean of the Battle-axe.

There is no 'correct' spelling of Maclean.

Variations have come about through error, illiteracy, translation from the Gaelic, personal preference, immigration clerk's preference or simply because spelling was usually phonetic and not standardised until dictionaries and printing codified it.

Most of the Macleans who visit Duart have a variation of the name Maclean. McLean, Maclean, McLean, Maclain, McLaine, MacLaine, Mclain and Macklane all make appearances in the Maclean guestbook. The most common sept to appear is Rankin.

No matter what your name is or how you spell it, everyone is welcome.

6 - SIR LACHLAN MACLEAN

'The stories would come out when the wine was flowing'.'

I'm Lachlan Maclean and I'm lucky to be the owner of Duart with my son Malcolm. We make up the Duart Castle Partnership which runs Duart, and includes the castle that is open to the public, the tearoom and the giftshop. The profitability of these businesses is key to the repairs that we're doing at Duart. With no profit we must cut the amount of work we can do.

I arrived back at Duart on the 17th March 2020. I had left Rosie, my wife, and Tilly, our dog, at our cottage in the south and I had intended to go down and collect them at Easter. Little did I realise that I wouldn't see them until October. The week that I got back to Duart, we went into lockdown. No one knew how this pandemic would develop. We were told by the medical advisers that about 20,000 people would die in this pandemic. We could never have imagined that the number of deaths in the UK alone would reach 125,000 to date.

I realised we were going to have to fight a war without being able to see the enemy. It was a very confused picture and all we knew was that the team at Duart would be shut down in our own bubble. The builders would have to leave and go home, and we wouldn't be able to see anyone except when we went for our food shopping in Craignure. Our bubble consisted of Alison and Ray who live full time in the cottage at Duart, Fiona who had come back to run the tearoom and Anne who had returned from New Zealand to run our shop. Andrew, my son, who had been isolating at his flat in Edinburgh arrived in early May.

My initial concern was about our business – would we survive? The government very quickly came up with financial help for businesses like ours and I was confident that with the reserves we had from the previous year we would stay afloat. I also realised that it was particularly important to keep everyone in our bubble briefed about what was going on. We set up our COBRA Meetings that were held on Tuesday and Thursday mornings. This would include the latest news about the pandemic and what we planned to do for the next few days. The meetings were named after the COBRA meetings that the Prime Minister has in times of crisis and as information was coming out from the government so frequently it was an especially useful tool to brief everyone as to what was going on.

It was from these meetings that Ray's idea of doing a video of us all during lockdown was developed. Short videos of what we were all doing were produced for each of us by Ray and Fiona. They kept Duart in the minds of the people who followed our Facebook page and were very professionally produced by Ray and Fiona. On a Thursday evening we met at teatime for some wine and cake. It seemed to be rather more wine than cake, and that was a wash up meeting with us checking what we had or hadn't done during that week and it gave us an outline for what we were planning to do the next week.

Our last social event of the week was to have a meal together on Sunday nights. Everyone cooked something but I have to admit my efforts were rather limited. One of the highlights was the pavlova made by Anne. We had our problems with this meal. Some of our bubble were vegetarian so I discovered a nut roast with no meat in it so they could tuck into that while the rest of us enjoyed a roast leg of local lamb.

After the meal we played a variety of games over the period of lockdown. We started with the general knowledge quizzes from the back of the Times newspaper, discovered that Ray and Anne knew rather more than the rest of us in these quizzes, but we never managed to complete them, so we decided to move on to play UNO. This is a card game for children, which could explain why it was so successful for our bubble. Fiona, who had never played it, ended up winning and the scores are still stuck on the fridge in the kitchen at Duart. I tended to lose quite often so I thought it was time for us to move on to something else and we moved on to building the Jenga castle. This is a game where players in turn take out a wooden brick hoping that the Jenga castle won't collapse. It became clear that I have rather large fingers and seemed to be the cause of the castle collapsing, one time into Fiona and Anne's wine, which caused them a lot of concern.

We all got to know each other quite well and the stories would come out when the wine was flowing. One story concerned me going down to the shop and tearoom each day. Anne, who was in the shop found this tedious as she often had a half cup of coffee on the windowsill, and I would ask her to take it back to the kitchen. Alison and Anne set up a message system when Alison was working in the ticket hut. Normally the message from Alison to Anne was 'the sea-eagle is coming' when I was leaving the castle.

One day I was walking down to the shop and just as I got there, I found everyone coming rushing out to see the sea-eagle – Anne had forgotten that the message meant I was on my way and told everyone in the shop and tearoom that they should come and see the sea-eagle flying over. It was only one evening in lockdown that this came out.

As the weeks went by we started thinking that we would open the castle. We could only do so when the government gave us permission and they eventually said we could open on the 15th July. At that stage we had been in lockdown for three and a half months so we started working out how we would open. Initially we didn't have a set date so we were just planning for the future. This needed some radical thought as the Isle of Mull ferry which is the main route for people coming to Mull from Oban, was only taking 200 passengers per journey, rather than in a normal summer when they would take 950 passengers per journey. We knew therefore that we were going to have many fewer potential visitors to the castle, and we decided that we would open with the staff that we had in our bubble and would open for 5 days a week from Sunday to Thursday and be open from 10.30

until 4pm.

We also decided we would not run our bus from the ferry to the castle as there would be so few foot passengers on each ferry journey. We could only sell takeaways from our tearoom and Anne found in the shop that many customers were not buying what our shop normally sold. When we opened on 15th July Andrew my son was still here and he had been doing all the mowing around the castle which was an enormous help. When he went back to Edinburgh, I discovered how much there is to mow and I didn't keep the grounds anywhere near as tidy as he'd managed to when he'd been with us. I was very sad to see him go because he was a good cook, and I missed his excellent cuisine.

We realised during lockdown that for once we had been well organised with our ordering for the shop and had asked people to deliver our stock in that week of 17th March so we found we had a lot of stock that we knew would be hard to sell. We upgraded and developed our online shop and lockdown gave us time to take photographs of a lot more products and to revamp our website. With the support of the clan and the public we managed to significantly increase our ecommerce sales and it would be fair to say that since lockdown ended it has been ecommerce that has kept the business going. So, thank you to all of you who gave us your support.

We found as well that a lot of 'dinosaurs' i.e., those who don't really understand online ordering, would telephone us to find out how they could go about it. I took a call from a gentleman who wanted to buy one of our Jack Murphy raincoats, the long ones that come right down to your ankles. Being rather inquisitive I asked him where he was telephoning from and he said Hastings in the south of England. Why, I asked him, was he buying a Jack Murphy raincoat from us on the Isle of Mull, and he gave 2 reasons, we were one of the only companies who stocked these macs on our ecommerce, and they were reasonably priced.

'Oh' I said, 'we should be charging more' and he said, 'yes you should, but only after I've placed my order'.

We've made some good friends from people who bought from us and I think Anne and Alison have provided a great support to people who wanted our products.

As lockdown ended and we started getting back to work we have continued meeting on a Thursday night to discuss issues that are important to the business. In March 2021 we still don't know when we will be opening for this year. It's unlikely to be before the beginning of May.

Looking back at our lockdown period I think our COBRA meetings, as well as our social meetings, made our bubble stronger. We discussed and debated issues much more fully. We all got to know each other better so when we did open, we all knew each other and could understand the issues that everyone had. I did say several times at the meetings that the Macleans had survived worse things than this pandemic and I was sure we would come out of the other end stronger, and I do think that's been the case.

7 – FEBRUARY 2020

Coronavirus is assigned the name COVID-19 by the World Health Organisation, France records the first death from Covid-19 in Europe, the UK has nine confirmed cases and onboard the cruise ship The Diamond Princess the first British victim to die from it is documented. The first case on the African continent is recorded in Egypt.

The next few days were windy and wet, which made a change because January is usually wet and windy on Mull. There is a stereotype that the British talk about the weather a lot, and it is true, because we have so much of it.

Because of the wind, rain, and bursts of sunshine, the outdoor furniture provided for visitors to Duart, like picnic benches and seats, are in the front line of attack by the elements and need to be brought inside and renovated during the closed season. One of my winter tasks is to store it in the garage. Five bench seats, six picnic benches, six bins, the dismantled ticket hut and various odds and ends get stacked in a space designed to accommodate a medium sized tractor.

While the castle is closed everything that has been crammed in has to be cleaned up and stained or painted ready for the next season, a task that is hampered by my inability to ask for assistance. I don't know why but asking for help comes hard to me.

Which explains why early in February I was to be found perched with one leg on the top of three wobbly picnic tables that were balanced one on top of the other. My other leg rested on an upended bench that was threatening to topple any second and force me into a position usually only achieved by gymnasts after years of training.

I had been trying to scamper over the tables to reach something placed against the back wall, and made the error of trusting my instincts, despite years of such calamity being a regular feature of my life. It is also the reason Alison has ensured I have generous life insurance.

I wasn't exactly stuck, it was just that any movement on my part would lead to dire and painful consequences. All I had to do was choose which of the array of medical attentions I would inevitably require, would be the least embarrassing. I had my phone with me but calling for aid was clearly out of the question and I was not keen on explaining to a doctor how I had managed to do the splits in mid-air and fallen on my face ending up with 'Woodcraft Picnic Bench' stamped into my forehead. I was slightly comforted in the knowledge that at least I had fresh new underwear on, although there was no guarantee it would survive my unintentional calisthenics.

I was contemplating leaping up and swinging from

the rafters like a swashbuckling hero of my childhood when the decision was taken out of my hands. The bench began its slow but inevitable slide away from my left leg and fearing catastrophe, I pirouetted away from my perch and landed safely between my two outdoor furniture adversaries. Inwardly I applauded my display of debonair manliness - right up until the point where the bench righted itself, with some force, against the back of my head.

Armed with the knowledge that I clearly possessed the agility of a panther, the reflexes of a cobra, and light concussion, I decided to forgo any more furniture adventures in favour of a cup of coffee and a nice sit down.

While the castle is closed I have a daily round, when I wander about the castle with a proprietary air checking everything is in order. Mostly it is routine, empty the dehumidifiers, making sure windows are shut or open according to the forecast and satisfying myself that no one has snuck in and stolen the CCTV system.

Even with the ongoing building works there are some areas where minor leaks are still a nuisance. When a potential source of a leak has been plugged by skilled artisans using handcrafted materials, the following day a tell-tale drip, drip, drip will mock them from elsewhere in the building.

It is a constant battle; one we are winning but it is taking time and patience. When the castle was a fully manned fortress capable of withstanding bombardment from land or sea the damp was less likely to have been a problem. Constant fires and people milling about kept heat in the walls, and anyway a bit of damp was a minor problem compared with finding your insides exposed by a sword wielding member of a rival clan.

Nowadays it is an issue though and the replacement of every bit of mortar between the stones is just one part of a huge job. If I think it's bad now though, imagine being in the castle in the winter of 2013-14 when four ceilings were brought down by water penetration through the chimneys.

Following the restoration in 1911 constant work and repairs have been a feature of the castle's recent history, including two major overhauls in the 1970s and 1990s.

In 2012 the Chief declared that the ongoing cost to make the building watertight was beyond his family's means. The Clan stepped up, an appeal was launched and Clan members, members of the public, grants from Historic Scotland and some family money have all gone towards the repairs and restoration.

It's still an ongoing project and one of the more frequent comments we get from visitors is about the scaffolding. It is a necessary evil really. The work is slow and methodical and moving the scaffolding is not a job for the faint hearted. It is a work of art though, the section on the rocky north east wall of the castle is already three stories high before it even reaches the castle walls.

A couple of years ago I was in the Sea Room when two women came in. We fell into conversation and it turned out that they were on holiday with their respective husbands. Apparently, they had seen the castle from the ferry and the women thought their other half's suggestion of a trip to 'that castle on the rock' was going to be a holiday treat. When they eventually got to the ticket hut the gentleman walked past and headed to the builders' compound and proceeded to take numerous photos of the scaffolding.

'They had no intention of coming in, they just wanted to take photos of the blooming scaffolding…' I was informed by one of the ladies. 'It's a lovely castle, but I'll be honest love, we only came in to spite them' her companion added.

As the month ended, we were increasingly tuned into the news as coronavirus started moving up the running order. The story from Italy was cause for concern, and we played around with different scenarios for opening the castle as we wavered between optimism and pessimism about the season ahead. As February faded into March, stock for the shop was starting to arrive to keep us busy and the work inside and out was beginning to look like we would be on target to get everything ready for opening.

All we needed was customers.

February 2020

Dry days 3,
Max temperature 12.1,
Min temperature -0.6.
Max wind speed 46.8 mph,
Monthly rainfall 16.53 mm

8 - TOROSAY

Across the bay from Duart is Torosay Castle, a stately home completed in 1858. It is surrounded by 12 acres of formal gardens and was once the seat of a 24,000-acre estate that comprised numerous estate workers and properties in the area, including the ruins of Duart Castle. In fact, Torosay was known as Duart House and sometimes Duart Castle, until Sir Fitzroy bought the ruins of the original castle back in 1911.

The gardens of Torosay are of particular note. They date back to around 1900 when the first features were laid out, including the formal terraces. Later additions include an oriental garden, a rockery, bog garden, a formal walkway with statues by 18th Century Italian sculptor Antonio Bonazza, water and woodland gardens and a formal walled garden.

Today Torosay Castle is owned by The Dew Cross Centre for Moral Technology, a charity registered in Scotland. The gardens are maintained by them and open to the public during the summer, presently on the first Sunday of the month between May and

October but do check first if you are planning a visit.

9 - ANNE CLOTHIER

'I can't work or live with you in the middle of nowhere!'

Hi, my name is Anne Clothier and I have been at Duart for over 4 years, with the last two years being the Retail Manager of the Duart Giftshop.

Well, what a year 2020 turned out to be. Certainly not what I or any of us expected.

I arrived at Duart in 2017 with my daughter Zoe, who stayed with me for the season as a Duart Girl in the kitchen area.

Going back a little further will show why or how I ended up on a Scottish Island from the other side of the world. It has been an experience that anyone of any age could really do if they choose to.

I grew up on the South Coast of the UK in a small village called Warsash. At 21 I trained as a nurse in Portsmouth and on one of our holidays I travelled with friends to the coast of Italy...where I met my future husband on a beach! A Mills and Boon style romance saw me move to New Zealand when I graduated. Many years and events later, saw me separated and the mother of three wonderful young adults deciding to visit an old nursing friend in the UK for her wedding.

I arrived for the summer after being away from the UK for 14 years as a visitor and 28 years as a resident! My sisters and children encouraged me to stay on and look for employment for a while. I found work at the Office for National Statistics a name which we have all become more familiar with since the Covid outbreak, giving, us statistics and info on a weekly basis.

The following March my two daughters came for a visit. We decided on a road trip so embarked on a three-week tour of Scotland and Ireland. We arrived in Oban during March, while everything was still on winter hours, so we never made a trip to Mull as I had hoped.

On heading home after an amazing trip, I started looking at jobs in Scotland. My daughter Zoe was planning to stay and look for work too. When I spotted a position for a couple in a Scottish Castle which seemed to fit our skill-set I suggested this to her.

'NO', she said. 'I can't work or live with you in the middle of nowhere!'

I had looked on the internet and Mull looked adorable with beautiful beaches. I thought it was so small that I could walk around it or to the major beaches in the evening. Turns out Mull is much larger than I thought.

A few days later my daughter, who was finding it harder than she thought to find a job for herself said, 'are you applying for that job?' So, we applied as a couple! As the season had already started, the Duart team needed more members for the season and the Clan Gathering that was imminent. We got the jobs, my retail skills and her cafe skills meeting the needs. So, from applying on a Thursday, we accepted the job on Monday and were on our way to Scotland two weeks later!

In reality we had no idea to where we were going!

Season one was amazing fun. A totally fantastic team of people both in and out of work. Junelle, Stuart, Alison, Kate, and Christina welcomed me into a fun team, being called Mom was lovely. Fun was had at Duart, down the local and all over the island. Having my daughter with me was wonderful. A chance to rekindle our relationship after many years doing our own things.

At the end of the season Zoe headed off to work for Top Deck Bus tours as an on the road chef. Over the winter we enjoyed amazing time together travelling to The Netherlands, Paris, Barcelona, Ireland and then Hong Kong on our way home. The best travel buddy ever, I thoroughly recommend having an overseas experience with your young adult child. I learnt so much about her and myself!

Season two saw me back at Duart again in a mixed role in the cafe, shop and the castle. Season three and four have seen me head home to NZ for the UK winter and return to Duart as the Retail Manager.

After an amazing year in 2019 we were so looking forward to topping that in 2020, but life was to challenge us this year.

I had spent my winter in New Zealand, enjoying a wonderful summer. Early March 2020 saw me heading to the airport with news of the Covid outbreak spreading across the world. I spent the first week with my family down south only to wonder what I should do. Italy was heading into a lockdown as the crisis became serious and close to home. I started to doubt what would happen in Scotland, would we open, would any tourism happen.

Mid-March saw me back at Duart in my mobile home, tucked behind the tearoom.

We started setting up for the season as the stocks started to arrive. As Boris the Prime Minister, and the Government started their Cobra meetings, we started ours around the Chief's kitchen table.

Twice a week, Sir Lachlan chaired a meeting with me, Alison, Ray and Fiona. Each meeting we discussed and reacted to the news coming from Holyrood and our first Minister Nicola Sturgeon. Our plans for opening gradually reduced from full opening to offering outdoor tours to eventually the news of the lockdown and the closing of the venue to the public. Who knew what, how or when we could open?

March moved into April, then May, June and with July approaching we started to plan for a possible opening! Adjusting our facilities to suit the restrictions was an experience. Building a screen in front of the counter. Sourcing hand sanitizer. Developing a one-way system to create a safe way of opening.

The above shows just how many weeks and months we were not trading. During that time, I turned up for work Monday to Friday to create online marketing for so many of our wonderful products that we had no physical customers to view. Amazingly you all supported us so well and kept me so busy packing parcels and sending them all over the world. The fun Duart Supporters pack was our biggest seller...many thanks everyone!

While we remained in lockdown, we became a family unit, in our own bubble up the hill at Duart. Each residing in their own space but coming together for our meetings, plus Friday night work drinks and Sunday night shared dinner. Incredibly the busiest social season I have ever had at Duart!

The weather improved and so we enjoyed wonderful weather as we explored the countryside around Duart. Although Mull is a small island, and we had all locked ourselves safely down, the rules said do not travel more than 5 miles for exercise. So, we drove to Salen for our shopping at the local Shop, queuing outside in all weathers and only enjoying a sneaky walk at a spot on that journey. It wasn't until our First Minister allowed slightly further distance to be travelled that I ventured to such wonderful spots as Lochbuie.

The island and the land around Duart during these times was so quiet. The skies even had no planes. The sound of cars in the distance was rare. Nature took over and enjoyed the reduction in visitors. We appreciated otters on the shoreline, deer grazing outside my caravan and the sheep stayed at Duart for months and dropped their lambs. We enjoyed them running around the grounds...we did not enjoy the number of droppings they left, which having no grounds person this year became predominantly the Chief's job...mowing and raking up animal debris!

Our Friday night drinks were a chance to laugh and enjoy the support and fellowship of our teammates. A chance to enjoy the comedy of our leaders and that of other leaders over the oceans.

Sunday night dinners was a chance to enjoy a great

meal and the opportunity to try new recipes that cooking for one would not usually prompt. Somehow, despite not being a particularly good cook, I became the queen of desserts! Each week I challenged myself to create something special and different, often reflecting my NZ adopted home. Favourites I am informed were Lemon Meringue Pie, Pavlova, Cheesecake and Ambrosia. Nigella's chocolate pavlova also went down so well! Try it!

Life before opening was strange. A chance to get to know my colleagues. Games after dinner on Sunday showed strange skills, from Jenga, Uno and topical quizzes. I know I am competitive but so are many of my colleagues! The eagerness to play another game meant late night finishing and an extra glass of wine. The fun of dodging my spilled wine as the Chief failed at Jenga once again.

Once the site opened life changed. Our bubble was no longer as safe, so we cut back on some of the social contact. Customers came to visit. Many adhering to the rules, a few with no idea! But most followed our rules and carefully looked around the shop or purchased their coffee and headed out into the poor weather! That was one of the saddest parts, not being able to offer a seat for visitors to enjoy their time at Duart. Many of the visitors in 2020 were from the UK. It was wonderful to see so many people who probably would normally head to Europe for their holidays. Sharing the wonders of Mull with these visitors is still such a joy to me.

After the season we packed up and continued to promote and send out so many wonderful products through the online shop. This kept me busy for weeks until I moved into a house sit in the village, hoping it would be cosier than my caravan. It has been lovely, but my fire lighting skills have not really improved! I have coped through the winter but having applied for a position back home in NZ over Christmas, in February I was offered the position. The chance to head home to my family and the relative safety of a country currently free of major outbreaks I jumped at the chance to become the manager of a country museum and event centre.

So sadly, I left Duart and Mull at the beginning of March 2021, flying home to NZ.

My time at Duart before and after Covid has been one of my life's most incredible experiences. The first year sharing the time with my daughter was amazing. The friends I made over the years will stay part of my life forever.

I will be back, probably not to work, but once more to enjoy the wonderful friendliness of an island that is now embedded in my heart.

10 – MARCH 2020

Italy's health care system struggles with more than a thousand new cases every day, and goes into a nationwide lockdown on 9 March. The WHO declares the virus a pandemic and the first signs of the global impact on the economy are felt as stock markets have their worst day since the 2008 financial crisis. The first positive case of COVID-19 is confirmed in Scotland at the beginning of the month and the first death 13 days later. The Scottish Government announces the closure of schools and nurseries and all pubs, restaurants, gyms and other social venues across the country are to close. Lockdown begins. People across the UK start a weekly clap at 8pm to thank the NHS workers and caregivers for their service in tackling the pandemic.

March started out fine. The weather was agreeably mild, Anne and Fiona had arrived and were settling in and the stonemasons and builders were beavering away in a noisy but productive fashion.

Under the stewardship of the Chief, we started to meet as a team. There was a season to plan for and as the month passed, we could sense the increasing likelihood of some disruption ahead. People were on edge, waiting for the news bulletins and grasping at little hints of hope or despairing at the weight of what may lay before us. We were all wondering if the events in Italy and elsewhere were coming to our shores.

We began to look at the coming season, now less than one month away, differently. Would we see a significant drop in numbers? What would happen to travellers from abroad? How could we cut back if we had too?

Decisions, decisions, decisions.

During the winter I had conducted some telephone interviews with potential staff from Hungary and France. Alison was in touch with a Maclean from Canada who wanted to work here for the season and the Chief was conducting negotiations with a young Maclean couple from Australia.

We had to decide, for their sake and our own.

Decisions, decisions, decisions.

There was no easy solution. If everything calmed down, we would need them, but the momentum seemed to be with Covid-19 so early in March we reluctantly agreed. We would manage with a skeleton staff to begin with and re-evaluate as the season progressed. Bringing people in, particularly from abroad was irresponsible and unfair to them if we ended up locked down. We also decided to delay getting our usual minibus to transport passengers from the ferry and back.

By mid-March there was a feeling of impending doom at Duart. Alison and I went to the mainland for a quick trip to meet friends and on-route we took a call from one of the Highland cruise ships that brings customers to us. They had decided not to operate for the whole season.

Phoning back with the news, we found out bus tour companies were cancelling their bookings too.

We returned to a gloomy castle, it looked bad. Nevertheless, although people were advised not to travel some tourism had started. I was in the grounds the day after we returned painting the logs that mark the boundary of the carpark. It was cold but sunny, the sort of dry brittle day that makes physical work outside almost a pleasure.

I heard the bus before I saw it, fortunately for its passengers because, judging by the nice cooling breeze, I was displaying a fair amount of, how do I put this delicately, bottom cleavage, in solidarity with workmen everywhere.

As the bus crunched to a halt in a series of hydraulic wheezes I wandered over and met the guide, a slightly manic chap who had brought his tour group to an island that was practically closed and now had a long wait for the ferry trapped with a bus load of restless customers. Feeling for his situation, I somehow convinced him that the sweaty and paint splattered specimen he was talking to was also an experienced guide capable of giving his group an erudite and witty introduction to the castle.

Which I then did. They applauded, laughed at the jokes, and asked sensible questions. I formed the opinion that they were starved of attention, travelling as they were on the cusp of an approaching pandemic.

When I had finished, they disembarked and had an amble around the grounds, where at least half of them tried the door to the toilets, despite me telling them they were closed because the water was turned off. I carried on painting as they clambered back aboard. My final view of them was watching the guide ricochet down the bus, bounce off several seat backs and disappear from view as it negotiated the tight turn out of the carpark.

Serves him right for not tipping, I thought somewhat uncharitably, and returned to my painting.

We adapted our opening plans so that we could be ready with three weeks' notice whenever we got the green light to open. Without saying it out loud we had acknowledged that opening on 1st April as planned was now very unlikely.

Tensions had been building through the UK and every evening we were all glued to the news. The First Minister begun daily briefings on 22 March 2020. We knew what was coming, but it did not lessen the impact.

On 24th March 2020 we began the first day of lockdown.

UK Prime Minister Boris Johnson announced that, *'people should only go outside to buy food, to exercise once a day, or to go to work if they absolutely cannot work from home. People will face police fines for failure to comply with these new measures.'*

First Minister Nicola Sturgeon stated: *'Let me be blunt. The stringent restrictions on our normal day to day lives that I am about to set out are difficult and they are unprecedented. They amount effectively to what has been described as a lockdown.'*

Later that month came the news that Boris Johnson and Health Secretary Matt Hancock had tested positive for coronavirus.

This was real.

March 2020

Dry days 4,
Max temperature 14.6,
Min temperature -1.6
Max wind speed 36.9 mph,
Monthly rainfall 10.61 mm

11 – COAT OF ARMS

You may be familiar with the coat of arms of the Chief's line. It's on display in several places in the castle, including carved into the fireplace in the Banqueting Hall, and on the flag that flies above Duart when the Chief is in residence and the castle is open.

In common with most Scottish heraldry it pre-dates the 1672 registration of arms, so exact meanings are lost in the mists of time. Plus, somewhat typically, the West Highlands of Scotland have their own way of doing things, and this extends to heraldry.

According to *'A Closer Look at West Highland Heraldry'* - by Alastair Campbell of Airds, Unicorn Pursuivant of Arms, 'West Highland heraldry is characterised by the use of quartered arms and by the repetitive use of one or more of a number of highly symbolic charges.

These are: The Lion Rampant, The Galley, The Hand and The Salmon.

This is what is recorded in the Lyon Register for

Maclean of Duart:

'Quarterly, 1st, Argent, a rock, Gules; 2nd, Argent, a dexter hand, fesswise, couped, Gules, holding a cross crosslet fitchée, in pale, Azure; 3rd, Or, a lymphad, her oars in saltire, sails furled, Sable, flagged, Gules; 4th, Argent; a salmon, naiant, Proper, in chief two eagles heads, erased, respectant, Gules'.

Just in case that's not clear:

Upper left quarter - a rock. It might have once been a castle. Some say it represents the Isle of Mull or Cairnburgh, in the Treshnish Isles, where the Macleans fled when Duart was taken by the Campbells in 1681. Another theory is that it's the rock upon which Duart stands.

Upper right quarter - a red hand holding a cross, is a reference to St. Moluag. He founded a monastery on the Isle of Lismore, just across the water from Duart. An early Abbot of the monastery was a relative of Gillean of the Battle-Axe. The red hand refers to an area now known as Ulster in Northern Ireland, which is where St. Moluag and Gilleain's ancestors came from. In West Highland heraldry they signify Christian evangelism. The name Gilleain in ancient Scottish Gaelic can be translated as Children of the servant of (St) John.

Lower left quarter – a black galley, officially known as a Lymphad, but also referred to as a Birlinn. The Birlinn is the old West Highlands galley, said to be based upon the Viking longship. Its use on the coat of arms means that the clan was affiliated with the Lord of the Isles.

Lower right quarter – In heraldic terms twin eagles

signify that the bearer is an individual of action and integrity. There is however evidence from the Exchequer Rolls to show that the Chiefs of the Clan Maclean once supplied hawks to the King, so it might have been a kind of royal endorsement. It was common practice in the West Highlands to show your political and military allegiance in this way.

In Gaelic cultures salmon represents eternal life because they return to their place of birth to spawn.

12 – ALASDAIR BARNE

'I had lost over a stone during the week.'

Although the tone of this book is largely light-hearted we can't ignore the fact that in 2020 an estimated 1,828,307[4] people lost their lives to Covid-19. Many more had symptoms that ranged from almost non-existent to severe and potentially life changing. Alasdair Barne is the Chief's nephew and both he and his wife Biz caught it towards the beginning of the pandemic in the UK.

He has been kind enough to share a few words about his experiences here.

Living with Coronavirus:

Biz was unwell at the end of March 2020 – we are not sure if our children had any symptoms either. We didn't think much of it because she was just exhausted and slept for three days, at that time Corona Virus wasn't such a big thing in the UK. She did lose all her

---
[4] Source. worldometers.info/coronavirus/worldwide-graphs/

sense of taste & smell and we both thought this was very strange. This was before it was a known or a confirmed symptom of the Coronavirus.

A day or two afterwards she felt better, but I felt like I'd been hit by a bus. I lost every ounce of energy and took myself to bed, and there I stayed for seven days. My temperature swung from 39°C to 40°C and at times 41°C, I was advised to take paracetamol every 2 hours to help keep my temperature down. It was like having flu where your whole body aches, but having even less energy than I've ever experienced. Even going to the loo took all my energy out of me and was the only exercise I could manage each day.

I drank every 2 hours with the paracetamol and ate the odd bit of toast but most of the time I just slept or was awake shivering with the fever. My chest felt weak with a slight cough but nothing that others now report when they have Coronavirus so I was lucky in this respect.

After a week I became a bit more awake and noticed I too had lost my taste and sense of smell. I had lost over a stone during the week and felt completely washed out. I am normally a highly active person, so it was a bit alarming. The next week I spent in bed still with 'outings' downstairs and in the third week I was able to get outside. It took in all about two months to feel back too normal again.

Biz and I continued for about 9 months to still have limited taste and smell with certain things smelling very strange even now.

13 - APRIL 2020

At least one million people around the world have been infected since the outbreak began. Confirmed deaths pass 50,000. The Scottish Government produces guidance for social distancing for businesses in Scotland and orders the closure of all retailers that sell non-essential goods and other non-essential premises. The personal use of face coverings during the pandemic is added later in the month. UK Prime Minister Boris Johnson is admitted to hospital with Covid-19.

Simply Stunning!

That was the Chief's verdict, and it was one we all agreed upon. It was late in the afternoon and we were gathered outside looking over the Sound of Mull. Ben Nevis and the mountains of the Glencoe range to our left and all the way around to the peaks of Ben Cruachan and Stob Diamh on the right. The sea was like a millpond, the island of Lismore reflected perfectly on the mirror like sea.

The sun was behind us and we threw long skeletal shadows over the freshly cut lawn. Every feature of Lismore and the mountains beyond was crystal clear and picked out in shades of lilac and purple in the translucent light of the sinking sun.

A buzzard floated lazily on the breeze, hardly moving as it scanned the ground below. The last ferry of the day was heading our way from Oban, cutting through the water and leaving barely a ripple in its wake.

Going back into the castle was a much bleaker prospect. Come lockdown the builders and stone masons had left. Everything was discarded pretty much where it had been when they had been working the day before they went.

In the Banqueting Hall a temporary wall had been erected in an alcove to protect the rest of the room from the work to replace iron beams. Behind it, floorboards were missing, and due to the unfinished work on the balcony above, rain penetrated and had to be channelled via plastic sheeting into a large bucket.

Such is the devious nature of water that as soon as it sensed I was familiar with its route, it changed its path and dumped a few gallons of rainwater somewhere else. I would then move the bucket to that point, whereby the whole game started again. It became a battle of wills between us, and I am ashamed to admit that by the time the holes were plugged I had been defeated by an inanimate element.

Although we rub along well, I am sure that if the Chief and I were interrogated there would be plenty of topics that we hold differing opinions about. But nothing divides us more than the culinary treat, in my opinion at least, of the fish finger sandwich. It is one of mankind's greatest inventions and should take its rightful place alongside the wheel, penicillin and space travel as a pinnacle of human endeavour.

I was halfway through this delight, with tomato ketchup oozing down my chin in a saucy and alluring fashion when a thump on the window jolted me back into the here and now.

Sighing heavily, I got up and went to investigate, thinking perhaps an eagle had flown into the window. Instead of a stunned raptor I found the Chief wiping his fist marks off the glass and calling out, 'Come on, we're about to start…now, where has Anne got to?'

Alison scurried past me and said, 'We forgot, thank goodness you reminded us.'

'I thought it was an earthquake', I mumbled to myself, as I left my half eaten fishy delight and grumped up the hill to join them. Anne came up from her caravan and the weekly clapping for NHS staff and other key workers began.

It was a curious phenomenon, but it captured the spirit of the nation at the time. People stepped out of their front doors and clapped, rang bells, bashed pots and pans, and generally acted in a socially acceptable antisocial manner for five minutes every Thursday, for 10 weeks.

Later during the weekly applause, we all took to parading down the road to see our neighbour Janet, who lived in a cottage a mile away. We would be banging pots and pans like a medieval pageant and arrive on her doorstep twenty minutes after the rest of the UK had finished clapping, looking faintly embarrassed. She was exceedingly kind and indulgent of the weird castle people with their quaint eldritch customs.

By now lockdown was happening in earnest. Movement was restricted to essential shopping, medical emergencies and exercise close to home of no more than 1 hour a day. We were fortunate to find ourselves in a rural location with an abundance of space and a community on Mull that rallied to the cause with commendable fortitude and optimism, even during the darkest of times.

With no prospect of the castle opening any time soon we took the exceptional step of shutting the grounds, which are usually open all year for visitors. This was unprecedented and heightened our sense of isolation. We put up a hastily written sign that I had scribbled, subsequently re-written properly by Fiona, informing people that the grounds were closed until further notice.

Except for the sheep, although we didn't specify that on the sign.

They were an unusual feature this year because they are usually allowed in during the closed season, then excluded from enjoying the lush greenery of the site during the times we are open to the public because of their fondness for 'fertilizing' the grounds.

Since we wouldn't be opening in the immediate future this meant the sheep could stay, it saved having to cut the grass and we had the extra treat of small lambs gambolling around.

We took great joy at watching them frolic and form a little gang who would race around the grounds chasing each other in a delightful fashion. In the warming rays of the April sun, during a difficult time, they brought us great happiness. Until that is, they discovered Alison's garden, but that's another story.

April 2020

Dry days 16,
Max temperature 22.1,
Min temperature -2.6,
Max wind speed 36.9 mph,
Monthly rainfall 2.09 mm.

Visitor numbers compared to April 2019 – down 100%.

14 - PARLOUR GAMES

One day, while in an area of the castle not to be disclosed, I found a duck. It was made of brittle plastic and had clearly been much loved but was now in a rather battered condition. Further investigation revealed that it had been placed in hiding for the Chief's grandchildren, or possibly even children, to uncover some years ago. It was returned to its hiding place where it still resides.

It's just one of a few childhood related goodies around the castle, or in one case presently missing presumed removed. One pocket of the billiard table used to house a small mouse, now sadly lost or pilfered by a light-fingered visitor.

Nearby, in a hidden location, is a copy of a song by Ada Leonora Harris, that starts:

> *"Tick! Tock!" says the old oak clock,*
> *"Tick! Tock! I'm you're grandfather's clock,*
> *For nearly a century here in the hall,*
> *With elbow grease glistening, stately and tall,*
> *I've stood, like a rock, with my back to the wall,*

Telling the hours aa they come and go:
Seldom a minute too fast or too slow.

Then there are the stilts. The Chief re-discovered these hiding at the back of a cupboard and revealed that they had been one of his childhood toys. He admitted that he had never been successful on them, preferring to roller-skate his way down the long corridors of Duart, much to his parents consternation at the time.

Despite my pleading he refused to try them out, but we might be able to find a place to display them one day.

15 - ALISON CANHAM

*'...In dressing gown and slippers,
chasing the sheep off up the hill!'*

I was born in Cambridge, England, and lived there for 40 years. For those who don't know it, Cambridge and the surrounding countryside is extremely flat. Human nature being such as it is though, we seem to want what we don't have, and I have always loved places with hills. Ray and I spent 9 months exploring the UK in our motorhome and fell totally in love with Scotland, so when an opportunity arose to work for a season on Mull we jumped at the chance. We arrived in 2017 and we've stayed ever since.

As well as loving hills, I've always been passionate about history and love visiting historical sites, stately homes and castles, losing myself in the stories of the people who have lived there, who have loved and laughed and cried within those walls. My son would always be dragging me away from reading every single word of information on the noticeboards, much preferring to get outside to scramble over the ruined walls instead.

I also have a rather chatty nature and enjoy meeting new people so to be honest, working in a 14th century castle and getting to talk to people all day, well, it's like every Christmas and birthday present rolled into one – I'm living the dream!

When lockdown hit, I found it quite difficult to adapt. I felt almost claustrophobic and trapped on the island. I feel energized by interaction with people and I found that not being able to go and visit friends and family, or to welcome visitors here was really tough.

One of the things that I did to pass the time though was to try my hand at growing vegetables. I knew I was missing people when I found myself trotting down to the greenhouse every day to 'chat' to the lettuces. It became a running joke when I confessed I'd named them. One day as I was heading down for my daily 'chat' the Chief was coming out of the garden and stopped me.

'I'm sorry to have to tell you' he said in the manner of a doctor giving unwelcome news, 'but I'm afraid Margery has been eaten by slugs.' Tragedy!

It wasn't just the slugs though, I was also battling the sheep. I had decided to plant flowers outside the front of our cottage and Ray had kindly built a chicken wire frame over them to keep them safe from marauding deer and sheep. Imagine my consternation one morning when I opened the curtains to see a sheep eyeing up a piece of lavender that was poking provocatively through the wire, having outgrown its protection. It was like the stand-off at the O.K. Corral.

'Don't you dare' I mouthed through the window, but the sheep looked at me and deliberately bit the top off the shoot and started munching. Next moment Ray saw me, in dressing gown and slippers, chasing the sheep off up the hill!

This is what happens when gripped by lockdown madness!

One of the joys of lockdown though, was being able to get to know the others better. In a normal season we are often so busy that we don't have a chance to really get to know our colleagues. But sharing meals together, having team meetings and time on our hands this year meant we all formed a strong bond. If one has to be locked down, it's lucky when you get to be with people you can feel relaxed and safe with and share some laughs.

Lockdown also provided an opportunity to explore the land around the castle and to see the seasons change in a way we hadn't had time to appreciate before. After a long, wet and windy winter we were blessed with a sunny, warm and dry spring. We watched the various flowers emerge, first the snowdrops and the yellow flowers of the gorse, the bluebells and irises exploding in the landscape in splashes of colour before the bracken unfurled and painted the hillsides green.

Seeing the birds return from their winter migration and build their nests, the lambs being born and growing up, having the time to sit and watch an otter playing on the rocks, all these things were such a pleasure and privilege.

I did, at times, find myself gripped by fear. I worried constantly about my parents, our sons and their partners, my siblings and their families, my friends. I felt that we were living in some apocalyptic drama, seeing the decimation of the human race (I can be a bit dramatic at times) and I was terrified of something happening to any of them, or to us here, and never being able to see them again. At times like this I would take myself off for a walk and find somewhere to sit and let the healing properties of the natural surroundings comfort me. I found rest in the silence, which wrapped around me and fed my soul.

As we emerged from lockdown and were able to welcome visitors back Ray and I were lucky enough to have some family and friends come to visit. Ray felt particularly lucky as it meant I had other people to talk to and he was able to take a break from my incessant chatter. I think he was grateful to finally be able to take the cottonwool out of his ears!

16 – MAY 2020

Scotland records the first weekly reduction of Covid related deaths, the UK Chief Medical Officers announce all individuals should self-isolate if they develop a new continuous cough, fever or the loss or a change in sense of smell or taste. The Scottish Government publishes information and guidance on Test and Protect and announces that the start of the route map out of lockdown is to begin at the end of the month. People in Scotland are permitted to venture outside more than once a day to exercise.

The evening was chilly and unusually dark. The grey clouds of day had given way to an impenetrable and starless black. The ceaseless wind that gathered pace as it funnelled between the mountains of Morvern and Mull was full of menace and spite and carried with it the scent of rain. At Duart it joined forces with gusts of icy north easterly wind from Loch Linnhe and crept into every nook and cranny of the castle, rattling windows and banging doors.

Lights flickered as the powerlines swung to the irregular rhythm of the breeze. Sheep huddled in the lee of the castle, bathed in the pale-yellow glow from a single light over the gate, the only bright point visible on this grim evening.

Inside, sheltered from the worst of the storm by a courtyard and walls built to withstand the harshest of Hebridean winters, six people were seated at the kitchen table. They had all followed their own path to the doors of this lonely fortress and each had a tale to tell about how they wound up in this forlorn outpost on such a desolate night.

At the head of the table, seated behind a half empty glass of Merlot was the Chief. The other five variously sipped wine, whisky, and IrnBru from Waterford crystal. Together these are the waifs and strays of Duart 2020.

Five of them have held the fort for over two months now. The locked-down quintet. The sixth joined them this month and has only just been let out of quarantine.

The Castle is shut. The exhibits remain wrapped up and secure in their winter hideaway. The tearoom and shop are empty, cold and forlorn. For the first time in living memory the grounds have been shut, with speedily written notices deterring visitors where cheery greetings should advertise opening times and special events.

There is a glint in the eye of the Chief tonight though. A sly twinkle as he shuffles the cards in his hand and surveys the room. He knows his opposition well by now, can identify the tell-tale tics and unconscious 'tells' each player displays, however much they try to hide them. A breeze seeps under the heavy kitchen door and the lampshade sways, illuminating five anxious faces waiting for his move.

Outside the rain starts, hammering on the windows and drowning out the hum of the fridge. The Chief rearranges his cards again, taking his time over each one, deliberately drawing out the moment and stretching the patience of his opponents. One finger taps lightly on the table, he adjusts his glasses and leans forward.

The rain has moved on, the wind subsides, somewhere an owl hoots. The lights flicker again…a chair scrapes on the concrete floor, a glass remains frozen halfway between the table and mouth. All eyes are on the Chief…

The world holds it breath.

'UNO!' He declares.

For anyone who is not familiar with the card game Uno, it is a simple affair targeted at anyone of five years old and over. The aim of the game is to be the first player to score an agreed number of points with a deck of special cards.

It was one of our Sunday evening post dinner pastimes. These started one evening when we had finished clearing the table and Alison had finished wiping me down and vacuuming the area around my place at the table. I am a notoriously messy eater, for reasons I've never quite fathomed. Food debris scatters around and dribbles down my front regardless of how much care I take.

Carefully sidestepping the wreckage of my meal, the Chief took some papers from the dresser and declared he had cut out a quiz from his daily newspaper for us to try.

It started well, but the questions got incrementally more obscure, and we found ourselves cursing our lack of knowledge about early Greek philosophers and Mesopotamian architecture. I think that is why he may have felt a card game in primary colours aimed at junior school children was more suitable for us.

Then we swapped to the more physically demanding Jenga. Jenga is the one where you build a tower from wooden blocks, then take turns removing them one at a time until it topples.

Despite what he tells you elsewhere, the Chief often did well at Jenga. He told us it was because he had decades of experience trying to keep a tower upright. When he failed, he did so in spectacular fashion, bringing the Jenga tower down into Anne's wine with the precision of a demolition expert dropping a factory chimney next door to a primary school.

The pre-games meals were a communal effort. Fiona would usually prepare a selection of vegetables, Alison and I would cook a roast, the Chief became something of a bread sauce wiz and Anne was the queen of deserts. Andrew would play the host, pouring drinks and preparing the table or taking over bread sauce duties when his father disappeared to fetch wine, answer the telephone, or embark on another search for his spectacles.

We experimented with different cuisines from time to time, with varying degrees of success. On curry night my Biriani was 99% rice, owing to my inability to understand the difference between cooked and uncooked weights. When roast red meat was called upon the others looked at Alison and I heartily tucking into out nut roast with a mixture of horror and pity.

Andrew Maclean had joined us during May. He was furloughed from work in Edinburgh and decided that a summer at the castle would be in order. Upon arrival he was whisked away to self-isolate. I was a little concerned for him because I had seen the Chief sweeping out the dungeons earlier that day, but as it happened, he was spared that and placed in a comfy room with its own facilities.

Every day for a fortnight we saw him taking his daily exercise and we waved to him from a safe distance.

Eventually he able to become a member of our bubble, joining in with Uno, for which he shared his father's passion. Indeed, it was Andrew who taught Fiona and I to play it. Fiona won the first hand and me the second, at which point he suggested Jenga instead.

May was turning out to be a hot one. The air was seldom still, but the breeze was light, and it was warm in the sunshine. I broke out my shorts, a legacy from days when such racy attire was practical, i.e., when I lived in the more temperate south of England. I discovered that they were made for a version of myself who had spent his days behind a desk or in a car and was therefore at least two waist sizes larger than the current model.

'I need a belt' I said to Alison, as my shorts fell down.

'Yes dear' she said, adding, 'I think I'll skip breakfast'.

Belt found, I tightened it to my new svelte midriff, causing the hems of my shorts to billow out at the knees. I then rummaged around in the back of the wardrobe for suitable summer attire to compliment my sartorial sophistication, settling on a purple tee shirt and orange sweater in case the early morning air was chilly. As the final coup de grace I pulled on my calf length work boots and bobble hat.

Alison looked me up and down…

'Darling' she said in the kindly voice she reserves for toddlers and puppies.

'Yes dear?'

'You know one of the symptoms of Covid is loss of taste?'

'Err, yes…'

'Do you think you should get a test?'

Attire adjusted and having narrowly avoided Alison spitting onto her hanky and cleaning cereal from my chin, I launched myself into my task for the day. Mowing the lawn.

We have a push along petrol mower that weighs more than a house and a ride-on mower that I used occasionally, but that privilege tended to be left to Andrew.

He was a natural and would chug up and down the lawns in his own world. The grass box on the mower was rather limited though and as soon as he had set off, I'd see him returning with a full load, a fact I remarked upon to him.

'I'm bringing the grass back one blade at a time' he said smiling from somewhere under his cap.

Most exciting of all gardening machinery though is the strimmer. I used to own one of those cheap electric ones you bought at the DIY store and used twice before the nylon unspooled or you diced a frog and lost all enthusiasm for the outdoor life.

The one at Duart is a serious petrol driven delight. For starters you must put on a special harness and helmet with a face guard. It all makes me feel like I am a bronzed Adonis with biceps the size of melons. When I take a rest and wipe my brow, I imagine the locals taking a break to watch me while panting and drinking an ice-cold diet fizzy soda whose name rhymes with poke.

Once suitably adorned in my safety wear the strimmer gets clipped into place to my midriff and I feel the warm tingle of testosterone flooding my senses, and away I go. At this point I struggle to start it, swear profusely and thanks to the ear protectors far too loudly, until it eventually gives in and chugs into life, suffocating me with malevolent fumes.

I now walk to the area that requires a good strim, where, without fail, it will stall. After another hearty swear and a light tantrum, I might manage to get it going and off I go again…

…Two minutes later either the nylon will stop feeding out and must be fed manually, which of course necessitates turning it off and, eventually, back on, or it will have run out of fuel.

With all these tribulations are behind me, I can spend a few hours merrily shortening nettles, bracken, grass, brambles, and the odd sheep[5]. In my mind I am a hero clearing mines in some post conflict mission of mercy or a modern-day buccaneer sweeping for buried treasure. In reality, I'm a sweaty bloke strapped to a lethal machine with a mind of its own butchering defenseless vegetation.

Unusually I got a touch of sunburn during May.

---

[5] Not really.

Normally I am impervious to sunlight anywhere away from the tropics. Alison can burn under an unshaded lightbulb, so she tends to slather herself in sun cream from March until November and makes sure I am protected too, which is nice but slippery and I do tend to smell like a coconut more than I would like. Given that Mull is often wet I've taken to explaining away my tan as rust.

May 2020

Dry days 14,
Max temperature 27.3,
Min temperature -2.2,
Max wind speed 39.4 mph,
Monthly rainfall 6.05 mm.

Visitor numbers compared to May 2019 –
down 100%.

17 – CASTLES EVERYWHERE

When the Macleans were part of the Lord of the Isles alliance of west coast clans, Duart's position was integral to its success and stood as part of a chain of at least eight castles, from Mingary at Ardnamurchan to Dunollie just outside Oban. These castles could send a signal to all the others if trouble was afoot by lighting a beacon fire.

Today you can still see Dunollie, and Mingary continues to guard the opposite end of the Sound of Mull.

The remains of Aros Castle sits on a dramatic peninsular between Salen and Tobermory and the walls of Ardtornish Castle are visible from Mull looking towards the mainland just to the right of Lochaline. Driving on the Morvern peninsular towards the tiny settlement of Drimmin you will find the remains of Caisteal Nan Con, the Castle of the Hounds, and eventually you may find the remains of the ancient Drimnin Castle, beside the Chapel of St Columba at, you probably guessed, Drimnin.

Mull's close island neighbour Lismore hosts the

evocative ruins of Castle Coeffin on its west coast and Achaduin Castle at its southern end. On a fine day you can see the remains from Duart, and its often quite distinct when you go past on the ferry.

On the east shores of Morvern, well into Loch Linnhe, is Glensander Castle, within the line of sight of Coeffin Castle and further north is Shuna Castle and Castle Stalker. Back towards Oban is the 13th century Dunstaffnage Castle. It is easy to see how the alarm could be raised in, for example, Mingary Castle and news travel down the Sound to Oban and possibly up Loch Linnhe too, all within a matter of minutes…so long as the guard was alert!

Moy Castle in the picturesque bay of Lochbuie was a Maclean stronghold, contemporary with the Macleans taking control of Duart, and at the north of the island is the mysterious ruins of Dun Ara Castle, close to the 19 century Glengorm Castle. These were not included in the signal chain as they are out of the line of sight of the other castles mentioned.

18 – ANDREW BRADLEY

'I didn't really have a clue what the job was about, but it did pay a wage.'.

Make it short he said, make it light, make it about how you came to be at Duart and how lockdown affected you. Well, that's fine for a published author to say but I'm a stonemason and my writing ability is sufficient to produce a contractor's report at the end of each month and tends to rely a lot on bullet points. Also, my typing is slow and laborious and has been described by my kids as 'like watching a bear type.'

So here I am, sitting in my static caravan at Duart (trailer for folks from the US) on a night of horrendous weather pondering on 'how did I get here?'

I guess the simplest way to explain why I am here is to say that my school career was not exactly stellar. I am 57 and I still look back with a certain amount of embarrassment on just how little effort I put into school. I left with basic grades, which were enough to let me apply to do a Building Surveying course. This was at the local technical college I should add, not university, that was way above my grade and above most people leaving my school in north east Derbyshire in the late 70s.

I was all set to go on my first week and had already been to the enrolment day when I got a call regarding an interview I had attended several months before, to be an apprentice stonemason. The recruitment had been delayed but now they had decided to offer me the job. I leapt at the chance to leave formal learning behind and take on my long-cherished dream of being a stonemason. Well not really, to be honest I didn't really have a clue what the job was about, but it did pay a wage.

I soon found out I was actually quite good at it; I enjoyed the physicality of it and the concentration required to carve large blocks of stone into complex shapes. I also did pretty well at the college in London that I was sent to for the theory side of the work. Ideas and methods that had made no sense to me at school suddenly became a lot clearer as they could be applied to something.

After a few years I got the chance to take part in the William Morris Craft Fellowship with the Society for the Protection of Ancient Buildings (SPAB). This was an amazing prospect which opened my eyes to all sorts of opportunities and allowed me to meet loads of interesting people whilst travelling the country looking at amazing projects, many of these people would reappear later in my career.

Shortly after completing the Fellowship, I was offered the chance to move to Scotland to run a training centre at a castle on the west coast. I stayed in this job for 18 years, got married and started a family. During 2003 the chance to take part in another Fellowship appeared, this one based in the USA, which I took and spent 3 months travelling up and down the east coast working with American craftspeople studying their methods and generally having a great time, I even got to work on the White House.

I learned so much about my craft during this time but after living so long in the same place we started to get the wanderlust again. My wife, a teacher, was offered a job as headteacher of a village school in the highlands. This meant that I was living in a place with no stonemasonry jobs within striking distance so I had to decide if I would remain at the training centre and travel home at the weekends or move on.

A chance meeting with another stonemason who I had met on the SPAB fellowship and who owned his own business led to me start work with his company based in Aberdeenshire. This was a very different kind of job with much more emphasis placed on management. I never really felt comfortable in a suit, but I learnt an enormous amount about the business side of the work, and I am still in awe of the work rate of the owner. He never seemed to sleep and no matter what time you got up in the morning and sent an email you always got a reply, I think 03:30 was the earliest, that was me getting up to travel over to Aberdeen for an 8am start and him probably having not yet gone to bed!

We did some big projects together and at one time had over 40 guys on site, with me looking after about 30 of them in the north of Scotland. I worked closely with my two contract managers Andrew and Steven and developed a great respect for their abilities.

These two would reappear at Duart in a different role some years later.

One thing that really sank in to me whilst doing this job was that no one can match the commitment of the owner of the company, having your name on everything and being ultimately responsible for all that happens gives an impetus that most employees cannot match. With that in mind and with an urge to go back on to the tools whilst I still felt fit enough I decided to become self-employed in 2012.

My idea was to work on my own carrying out small projects and enlisting the help of some of the great crafts people I had met over the years when I was faced with a job too big for just me. I was busy and enjoying life but probably missed the larger projects more than I admitted to myself. During 2015 I was contacted by an architect who had done the SPAB Scholarship, this was the professionals equivalent of the scheme that I had done, and we had met up a few times over the years as we were both living on the west coast.

He asked me if I was interested in tendering for the work at Duart Castle. It was a larger project than I had intended to take on, but I felt that there was also an opportunity to pull together some of the amazing people that I had known over the years and to take on a project in a different manner to many that are carried out in the normal hustle and bustle of contracting.

So, I found myself leading a small team of independent crafts people during the various phases of work at Duart. It's a small team as there aren't that many people in Scotland with the skills to carry out the work. They are mostly small companies or sole traders, as I prefer the guy with his name on the letterhead to be the one who is on the scaffold, and they are all friends.

Andrew and Steven who had been my contract managers had recently left the big company and were setting up a firm on their own and Duart became their first project. Darren and Jonny came on board to do the joinery and whilst Darren left to work abroad Jonny is still here. Jonny introduced me to Behzad, a painter and decorator and general builder from Iran who has one of the best work ethics and cheeriest personalities I have ever worked with. To carry out the roof and lead work we have Stephen, director of a company based in inverness and still on the tools. It's fair to say that Stephen or Murph as he is known, is held in high esteem by Sir Lachlan as he is a Maclean!

It was this team that were living and working at Duart during the early months of 2020. We watched the news in the evening of the unfolding crisis in China and talked about whether it would affect us. We didn't really believe it would.

Then it did.

We spent a couple of weeks trying to work in a socially distant manner, then one evening sitting watching the news (in separate rooms) the Prime Minister told us that we would all have to stop work the following day.

We had already realised that a lockdown was imminent so had spent a couple of days closing the site down, putting up temporary protection over the work still to be completed and generally making everything safe. On the afternoon of the 24th of

March, we wished each other good luck, didn't shake hands, and went home.

Apart from holidays, occasional colds, and a memorable occasion ln 2018 when I fell off a ladder at Duart and spent a few days on a ventilator, then three weeks in hospital, I have never been out of work. Lockdown was a bit odd and strangely enough I quite enjoyed it.

I do not mean in any way to be disrespectful to people who have struggled through lockdown but having three months off in the Highlands with my family allowed me to take a breath and catch up on things which I had not had time for, mostly in the DIY department. My daughter had come home from university and my wife was working from home, so we slipped into a rhythm of work, exercise, watching the Covid Briefings on TV, baking, and watching innumerable repeats of the American version of The Office, courtesy of my daughter.

Due to the ladder incident, I was supposed to shield as I am classed as vulnerable but in June when we got the word to go back to work, I decided I would go, partly to get away from any more episodes of The Office and partly as I had slipped through every financial safety net the Chancellor had flung out, I didn't think the risk was particularly great, I mean how much more socially distant can you get than being stuck up a scaffold at Duart?

So here I am back to the caravan again, still living through a smaller lockdown, vaccinated, and working with Behzad in a socially distant manner trying to do five men's work with just the two of us and still not quite understanding how I got here.

19 – JUNE 2020

The Scottish Government announces new public health measures to help suppress Covid-19 and prevent new cases being brought into Scotland. They also publish guidance to support Scotland's tourism and hospitality sector to reopen safely in July, if the virus is under control. The UK Government announce clinical researchers will begin human trials of a new coronavirus vaccine. By the end of June half of civilization has been in, or is in, some form of quarantine, which appears to have resulted in cases of Covid-19 falling significantly, and countries begin rolling back restrictions on businesses and travel.

With the castle closed and no visitors we had decided that we needed to keep contact with the outside world. Apart from shopping locally for essentials and walking for our daily exercise we seldom left Duart. The on-line shop was still ticking over, so we made occasional trips to the local post office with parcels to dispatch and during a COBRA meeting this gave us an idea. Homemade videos for social media to remind people that the castle was still here.

We started making them in May, and they ran weekly through May to June, with a bonus out-takes reel and a couple of extra information videos shot in the castle with the Chief explaining about some of the exhibits.

Fiona was a wiz with a camera, and so we decided to start with a video of the Chief in the castle showing the extent of the works inside and how it had all been left when the builders had to pack up and leave. Then we would all take turns to have our own video showing what we were doing during lockdown.

We started filming with two phone cameras, Fiona doing the main shooting and working out things like lighting and how to frame the shots, and I would be getting supplementary footage. Well, that was he plan. Somehow, I don't recall how or when, probably when I'd popped out of a meeting to use the lavatory, I'd been 'volunteered' to introduce each one.

So, I found myself in front of the camera, initially in an awkward stuttering introduction with so much nervous hand movement it looked like I was trying to introduce the Chief while indulging my passion for invisible knitting.

Anne was next up, telling everyone about the shop and boosting our online sales. Then Carol showed us around the garden where we grow a lot of the produce for the tearoom, which had all been planted in anticipation of a regular season. Alison was joined by the 'film crew' for her commute to work – all of 53 steps, and Fiona baked two metres (the recommended social distance measure at the time) of shortbread.

By this point I think we were going a little stir-crazy. My introductions were becoming less scripted and more, well daft would not be an exaggeration. Perhaps the most remarked upon was when I introduced Alison's piece from our kitchen in the cottage while wearing an apron that appeared to give me the naked chest of a body builder and the tight shorts of one of the Village People. What viewers did not know was that it was the Chief's apron that I had borrowed for the shoot.

You can find the videos at:
facebook.com/DuartCastleIsleOfMull/videos/

Towards the end of June, it was becoming clear that some sort of re-opening of visitor attractions could happen in July, so long as the course of the pandemic continued to slow down.

Across the island businesses were looking at the coming season, and a fair few decided not to open at all. It presented a dilemma for us, what to do for the best? After discussion and debate we decided to open, but in a restricted and careful way.

Operation 'open the castle' had begun.

The shop would open at the same time as the castle. We had no idea about what sort of visitor numbers to expect, and restrictions on catering venues prohibited re-opening of the tearoom until we knew more. We agreed upon ways to re-route visitors around the castle to minimise contact and a similar way of coping with the shop and toilets.

To help visitors navigate the areas where they might cross each other's path or if passing was impossible to avoid, the stairs for example, we devised a system of signs based on road traffic lights. Red for stop. Yellow for look and listen. Green for go

- when it is safe to do so. We felt this system was pretty much universal and would be recognised by guests wherever in the world they came from, although in truth we expected very few from abroad.

It seemed simple, effective, and as a bonus we could use the Maclean of Duart dress tartan for the red and Hunting tartan for the green.

Which left the middle as a simple boring yellow circle…for now.

In the meantime, we had all taken on projects to keep us occupied during lockdown. Fiona is trained in photography and art and could indulge in both. Anne got stuck into all things crafty, and produced various knitted garments, tea cosies and hats. Alison discovered the mysterious and dark delights of gardening with help from Carol, and I decided to put my music collection to good use and started a small radio station for Mull; called Mull Broadcasting. It wasn't a radio station in the truest sense of the word, more like a podcast with loads of music, some regular contributors and special guests.

It ran for 17 weekly shows from April to July 2020, plus a Christmas special in December. I had help from a lady called Gill who lives in Tobermory and who took care of organising other contributions, leaving me to concentrate on the music. We had poetry, people from around the world giving us an insight into life under lockdown where they lived, stories from Tobermory author Yvonne Marjot and Mulls own Alasdair McCrone read us a chapter of Neil Munro's *Para Handy* books every week in his inimitable style. The quality of the contributors made me sound exactly like the amateur DJ that I am, but I remain proud of our own tiny contribution to Mull surviving lockdown.

I included some wonderful music by artists who were struggling with not being able to perform in public, a mainstay of their profession. So, if you'll indulge me for a moment (and as you've read this far you are indeed a pretty indulgent and delightful human being) do please take a little time to seek them out:

Scotland's own Dean Owens; poet and songwriter extraordinaire Phil Burdett; Songdog; The Screens; Ags Connolly, and Adrian Nation, who is unique among the roster of guests as he has performed at Duart Castle and has since moved from Essex to Scotland and now lives on the mainland a few miles from Oban. They all have an online presence so have a search and give your ears a treat.

While we're at it, give your eyes and brain a treat and try Andy Brackens books, which kept me amused during lockdown. Worldly Goods or A Different Mix are good starting points.

Back at Duart Castle the end of June was beginning to feel tense. While we had it relatively easy at a remote and picturesque spot, with plenty of space and wildlife to entertain us, the separation from family and friends, and lack of other diversions was beginning to tell.

In some ways it seemed self-indulgent to be in such a spot and still feel sorry for ourselves. After all many were surviving in much harder conditions, including city flats and single rooms. Numerous people had lost loved ones or were fighting Covid themselves, and emerging evidence was showing that a lot of people's mental health was being affected by the lockdown.

Many were home-schooling fractious and bored children; those children were missing vital learning and socialising opportunities and some people barely saw anyone for months.

We could count our blessings that we had a structure to our week thanks to our regular patten of get togethers, but still some days were hard. Of course, there was the ubiquitous Zoom (other video networking software is available...) which kept us in contact with our loved ones in a fuzzy kind of way, but nothing could replace hugging your friends and family.

The care and support network on Mull was, indeed still is, simply marvellous. People went out of their way to support their community. I am sure it was a pattern repeated around the world, if any good has come from the pandemic it has been the extraordinary generosity and selflessness of so many.

Up to June even popping over to Oban had been all but forbidden unless it was in exceptional circumstances. The ferry timetable was cut right back to a lifeline service but at the end of June travel opened as restrictions were eased and we felt relieved and anxious at the same time. Shopping in Oban meant a greater variety of food, a chance to buy clothes and odds and ends that, great though the shops on Mull are, were something different.

It felt peculiar to be queuing outside the supermarket and then let loose in the brightly lit cave of wonders packed with a bewildering selection of produce. I was charged with the Chiefs shopping while Alison went around separately, choosing from

72 types of breakfast cereal, fruit in abundance, and vegetables we thought were the stuff of legends. She had to go and fetch another trolley just for the cheese aisle!

Back home and fighting off a diary coma we took a call from Andy who confirmed that he would be returning to check on the site, undertake a health and safety assessment and plan for the imminent return of Behzad and Jonny.

Carol had surpassed herself during the spring and the polytunnel, a sort of plastic greenhouse much favoured in these parts, was brimming with lettuce, spinach, beans, and that most horrendous of root vegetables, the beetroot. Yuk! Still, we had plenty of lettuce and started giving it away until people saw us coming and hid in case we would try and inflict more greenery upon them.

Alison had caught the gardening bug during lockdown, she even subscribed to a monthly magazine of horticultural pornography and the outside of the cottage is still awash with colour and greenery that she is rightly proud of.

I on the other hand, planted birdseed in our back garden when I was seven years old, and skipped downstairs the following morning expecting to greet a crop of budgerigars. I was disappointed then and have done nothing but the basics outdoors ever since. 'If it is not lethal - I am not interested' is my gardening motto. Hedge trimmers with trailing electric cables - check. Lawnmowers with bits missing - check. Sledgehammers that could drive a fence post through one's foot and into concrete - check. Tiny little scissors to remove single leaves, nope. Not I.

All in all, we were getting there, it felt like there

was some momentum towards normality, or at least a reasonable approximation of it.

June 2020

Dry days 10,
Max temperature 27.4,
Min temperature 4.1,
Max wind speed 39.4 mph,
Monthly rainfall 5.31 mm.

Visitor numbers compared to June 2019 – down 100%.

20 – GOING UP AND DOWN.

Duart has several staircases, including a narrow spiral stairway on the private side with an arrow-slit window that has its own built-in seat, allowing an archer to sit down in relative comfort and safety while shooting invaders.

There are a total of 87 steps to get from the drive to the top of the great tower, and one step down into the courtyard, and a couple of additional half steps if you are counting thresholds. 56 are spiral stairs.

At one time the Chiefs House, on the right of the courtyard as you enter, held a flight of outdoor steps to the first floor. The stone supports, called corbels, still jut out of the restored wall. There is a further set of corbels above the original entrance to the keep from what is now the Sea Room. These are hidden from view nowadays by the roof. They once supported a platform with holes in it that allowed defenders to rain down all manner of sharp or otherwise unpleasant things on anyone trying to force entry into the castle keep.

An added obstacle for potential invaders was the

inconvenient fact that the door to the keep was on the first floor. Neither the Sea Room nor the stairs to it existed until the restoration in the early 20th Century. Originally wooden steps that could be pulled up in the event of the courtyard being breached led up to a small platform. Later this area became a gun platform for cannon. Prints of the Castle done in the late 1800s show a small spiral stairway leading to the area that is now the Sea Room on the northeast corner. All traces of it have now been lost in the passage of time and the 1911 restoration.

21 - FIONA STEEL

'I had witnessed first-hand the horror of panic buying…'

The year I washed up at Duart was 2018. Originally from mainland Scotland, on the West coast, I always knew I wanted to spend a period living in the Hebrides. This was mainly due to my passion for nature and, the unrivalled landscapes of these locations. The Isle of Mull, being a favourite of the islands, seemed a good place to start. I took up a position within the castle tearoom not long after graduating and, inadvertently found myself still there in 2020. The year which would shadow all the previous.

Everybody's experience of the pandemic has been unique, although the initial rapid rate at which circumstances evolved is probably shared by most. I remember standing on the castle steps as our builders, working on the castle restoration project, packed up and retreated, becoming a smaller and smaller speck as they drove off down the winding road. We had just been put into national lockdown, I didn't know when I'd see them again. Surprisingly at this point, there was the idea that the lockdown might last only three weeks. However, it was apparent to me, that whatever was coming, would have a significant impact, stretching further than the first few weeks of spring.

I had recently just returned to Mull having spent the winter on the mainland, and this lockdown was inevitable. I had witnessed first-hand the horror of panic buying, with the shops rinsed dry; toilet roll, pasta, bread, milk, all being sold on social media to the highest bidder. Italy was then the pandemic hotspot. This was frighteningly close to home, no longer a world away on a distant cruise ship, we weren't going to escape. I had never intended to spend lockdown at the castle, but here I was. The following is a small insight into insignificant moments which have become my precious Duart lockdown memories.

The first few days I mainly spent glued to the news and, probably in a state of shock at the events unfolding. This rolled into weeks of endless phone scrolling and government daily briefings, bombarded with constantly evolving information, weighed down with figures and a need to 'flatten the curve'.

The antidote to this was to be found outside, in the landscape, surrounding the castle on all fronts. Day by day, the birds were awakening from a winter gloom, calling louder and longer, defending territories and looking for a mate. They became the background soundtrack to days which blended into one and, there was one bird which especially illuminated the darkest of these days, the song thrush. For a bird on the UK red conservation list, Duart has an abundance of them. I would set my alarm prior to sunrise, to time with the dawn chorus, and wander through the millennium woods to the sound of their extensive, repetitive repertoire, smiling all the way. They were soon joined by rousing robins, blackbirds, chaffinch, wrens, all competing for the loudest bird title.

Usually, as I walked back to the cottage to grab another hour or two's sleep, a pair of hooded crows would make their presence known by calling from the battlements, with the backdrop of a perfectly glowing sunrise, a promise of another impeccable spring day. At moments like this, it was unfathomable to imagine the horrors unfolding elsewhere. However, it was always accompanied by a sense of guilt. Starting and ending the day to this spring song and relative freedom was a real privilege, and one of which I was always aware. While the rest of the country was occupied with a sitting room workout with fitness guru Joe Wicks, or a home haircut, I still had the privilege to roam mile upon mile without another soul to be seen and, as for the self-grooming, well what was the point, nature didn't judge my unruly hair.

Another lasting memory came at 8pm every Thursday. Although the castle has no direct neighbours, we still rattled our pots and clanged our pans, along with the rest of the nation as we showed our gratitude and clapped for the NHS. The first evening of this was in complete darkness. Soon it was to open skies, biting midges and the calling cuckoo. This event crept around quickly, never seeming like a full week since the last time, and they swelled in significance. Eventually passing ships and our ferries both at Craignure and further in Oban could be heard blasting their foghorns. This felt very special, and it was a weekly reminder of the world around us.

It could have become all too easy, insulated in our bubble, to lose consciousness of the tragedies happening across the globe; hearing the ferries genuinely warmed my heart. Eventually these evenings were accompanied by the low flying swallows which return from South Africa every year to build their nests in the Duart outbuildings, the only international visitors we would see for a while.

Additionally, my weekly venture to the local shop became a day to look forward to, as it proved another channel to the outside world. On the way, I would momentarily stop at the ferry terminal to ponder over the empty car lanes. Usually, the Duart bus would be lined up waiting to collect visitors. There would be a waxing and waning of hustle throughout the day, but now crew undoubtedly outweighed passengers on the MV Isle of Mull. I would then head north to Salen. Being a small shop, there was always a queue formed outside. I would listen to the going-ons and opinions regarding lockdown. It was in this shop I learnt the schools would be closing; it's little insignificant facts like this I will remember of this time, the when and where. If there was ever more than four people before you in the queue, you had made the mistake to come at a peak time. The hour long waits to enter the shop and the panic buying never really made our shores. On return from my shopping trip, I would normally unpack a weeks' worth of dinners, but in cake form. I think they called that lockdown comfort eating.

In an attempt to justify my heavily iced treats, I would regularly swim in the sea surrounding Duart.

Although, I think the mental benefits far outweighed any physical. Some evenings the sea was rippled by a gentle breeze, on others, waves would break with the shore. However, my favourite conditions to swim were when the water surface was flat calm, almost surreal and hypnotic to watch. The surrounding hills and dark pink of the sunset would reflect on the water all around me, like swimming in the sky. Curlew and Oystercatchers would soundtrack this event, along with the slowly lapping waves. On one occasion, the faint chords of a guitar could be heard drifting from across the bay, carried in the peaceful air towards my ears along the Sound of Mull. My own personal concert, the musician unaware.

Other times, a little dark face would appear further out in the depths, curiously glaring me. It would disappear briefly, only to return, eyes still staring at mine, but from a further distance. I'm not sure if it was the same common seal every time, but I like to think that it was, my lockdown swimming partner. On these occasions I witnessed some of the finest sunsets, and always emerged from the salt sea feeling elated. On walking back to the castle, bats would skim my head, startled deer would prance alarmed from the undergrowth, and my nostrils would pick up the coconut sweet of the gorse, fading along with the light.

A year on, sitting at my desk writing these words, but now with rain battering across my window, in a more predictable Hebridean fashion, lockdown feels simultaneously like yesterday and decades ago. Both a dreamlike bliss, and a nightmare, the highs and lows were extreme. For me, nature is the years punctuation, and I like to ingest and process every changing moment, ingraining it onto my brain before it passes and is lost forever.

At Duart, the weather we experienced during lockdown was sublime, but not typical; sunburn in April, June and July. This added to that dreamlike quality. However, there was always an underlying sadness, not just directed towards the pandemic, but an acceptance that not all the passing phenomena of nature could be appreciated to the full, an admission that 2020 was not the year to absorb.

Duart certainly is a mysterious place, grounded on its black rock, and the experience of spending this astonishingly strange time here has not been lost on me. My memories may not live up to the drama one would expect from living in a castle, but I found my relief in the landscapes surrounding Duart during the uncertainty, and these moments I will always cherish. If, like me, you appreciate the natural environment, I'd recommend a visit, it won't disappoint.

22 – JULY 2020

The five mile limit travel in Scotland is relaxed, face coverings are made mandatory in shops and heritage attractions. First Minister Nicola Sturgeon announces the move to Phase 3 of the Scottish Government's route map out of lockdown which includes the reopening of visitor attractions from 15 July. The University of Oxford publishes its findings from a coronavirus vaccine trial, noting that the vaccine appears safe and triggers an immune response. More than 100,000 people are expected to take part in the next stage of the trial.

This was it; we were nearly there.

We made the decision to operate on reduced hours and only open for five days a week. This meant we could open with the minimum number of staff. It was a compromise between opening for longer - and saving money.

A decision like this was not taken lightly. One of the consequences was that it meant not employing people who would usually be part of the castle team. This was hard, the consequences of the pandemic reached further than just the physical. People's livelihoods were affected and Duart was just one tiny speck in the world.

We went through our plans, the route we had devised around the castle, tearoom, and shop, and we tested everything. Bottles of hand sanitiser and dispensers arrived, Alison printed signs and notices, Anne sorted the shop so people could browse safely and preferably without touching. She had a quarantine area set aside for clothes that had been tried on, and Fiona was on standby to open the tearoom when circumstances allowed. In the meantime, she would be helping at the ticket hut on the days when Alison was working as the Chief's PA.

The sheep were gone from the lawns, the bins were out, picnic tables and benches in place, tills were switched on, floors scrubbed, and signs put up.

And finally we put the ticket hut up.

This is an annual job that involves brute force, ignorance, and an industrial screwdriver, all of which I have in abundance. Fortunately, Jonny and Behzad were on hand to lift the roof on, which I have found from experience is a lot heavier than it looks. I took my place inside the shell of the hut to guide it into place while outside the real workers lifted it with deceptive ease and, working blind, slid it onto the shell.

The front of the hut is 1.7 metres high. I am 1.9 metres in my work boots.

'Is there something stopping it Ray?' Jonny asked.
'Yes'
'What is it?'
'My head'
'Can you move it?'
'Not right now, could you perhaps back up a bit?'

My last job was to strap it all down. The hut gets firmly anchored to the floor; a feature often remarked upon by customers.

The wind at Duart can be amazingly strong to start with, and then it gets funnelled between buildings so that the side of the hut gets buffeted with everything it has. When the gale is joined by its chum the rain the ticket hut looks like a spaceship re-entering the earth's atmosphere. It has ended up on its side in the past. Until the straps were added the person selling tickets was also employed as ballast.

We had one final COBRA meeting where everything was finalised. I's dotted and T's crossed. The Chief, who had donned his Maclean tartan trews for the occasion, stood up to make some announcements.

First order of business was to tell us that we had been awarded the VisitScotland Good to Go standard, which meant we could proudly display a certificate to reassure visitors that we had done everything practical to make the site safe for them.

Secondly, he thanked us all for our hard work to make the site ready to receive guests and for making the last few months as enjoyable as we could.

Lastly, he adopted a solemn demeanour, cleared his throat, and peered at us over his spectacles...

'Now...' he said, 'before we open, we're going to have a final treat...'

We were all uncharacteristically silent with anticipation.

'It's time for...'

We leaned forward in our seats.

A pause as his gaze swept the table, making fleeting eye contact with us in turn…I was afraid Alison may faint…

'…A poo picking party!'

Unfamiliar as the rest of us were to a fee-paying education or the private ways of feudal barons we waited for an explanation, with expressions that ranged from mouth agape stunned to puzzled frowns.

'The sheep poo' he explained, after a wicked spell of silence. 'It needs to be cleared and as it has been sunny it'll be easy. We don't want people turning up and having to wade through it.'

If I may be permitted a brief observation here, sheep do appear, to my untutored eye, to be little more than woolly digestive tubes on legs. They are certainly unencumbered by intellect. When the queue formed to give out brains, sheep were still in the eat-grass-all-day-and-grow-your-own-sweater line. I think they gave up after that and, well, went to eat grass. I don't know if it is possible to house train a sheep, but I suspect it would be akin to shouting at the wind to stop blowing.

In truth Fiona had already been a bit of a hero on the poo removal front and had already cleared quite a bit. With rakes, spades, and boxes the rest of us went forth and gathered what remained. Apparently, Carol would be able to use it in some arcane ritual that only true gardeners and eighth level wizards are privy too.

Suddenly, all talk of sheep deposits was set aside. Anne was hurrying to get everything ship shape in the shop, the castle was getting a last-minute spruce-up and the grounds were trimmed - customers were due.

We opened the castle and shop doors on

Wednesday 15th July 2020.

We were confident that we would get a few visitors as Alison had been fielding enquiries for a while and the grounds had been used by an increasing number of people since lockdown restrictions were eased, with people leaving and others arriving to begin their vacations.

We were open for two days then closed for the Friday and Saturday. These were the days when visitor numbers were usually a bit lower because they were traditionally change-over days on the island.

We had a handful of guests in the first two days. Those first customers were exceedingly kind and helpful with their feedback. Their experience allowed us to refine our approach and gave me the opportunity to perfect the small presentation I was giving to everybody when they came in.

Sales in the shop were steady and generally people seemed happy to find somewhere that was open and safe.

We were back in business!

July 2020

Dry days 13,
Max temperature 22.5,
Min temperature 5.0,
Max wind speed 27.15 mph,
Monthly rainfall 5.54 mm.

Visitor numbers compared to July 2019 - down 88%.

23 – LOCATION, LOCATION, LOCATION

Three major feature films have been shot at Duart.

The first was the 1945 Michael Powell and Emeric Pressburger film *I Know Where I'm Going*. It starred Wendy Hiller and Roger Livesey as the romantic leads and Duart as Castle Sorne. The film featured a 12-year-old Petula Clark, who went on to have a successful career as an actress and singer, including her 1964 Grammy winning song Downtown.

Next came the 1971 feature *When Eight Bells Toll*, an action-packed James Bond style romp based upon Scottish author Alistair MacLean's 1965 novel of the same name. It featured a young Sir Anthony Hopkins as the hero. Duart features in several scenes, although a boat house and waterfall are both studio tricks.

Then in 1999 *Entrapment* featured Duart as the base of an international art thief played by Sean Connery, whose mother was a Maclean, and Catherine Zeta-Jones as an insurance agent sent to catch him. Most of the inside scenes were shot at

Pinewood Studios in Hertfordshire, but the courtyard, battlements and grounds of Duart were all used.

24 - JONATHAN SCHIAVONE

'If you are committed, you cannot fail.'

My name is Jonathan, but everybody at Duart calls me Jonny. I am originally from Italy, from a small village north-west of Milan. A beautiful area rich in culture, with stunning landscapes and resourceful territories. We can call it countryside, and the name of the area might be translated in English as 'the land of the seven lakes.'

It is a bit different from the Scottish countryside. Life is quite frenetic there, as most villages and towns were born and raised under industrialised Milano. There are still trees and woodlands all around, lakes and streams, you can hear the birds chirping and sometimes spot a fox crossing the street at dawn. One day destiny led me to Scotland.

I moved here in 2014 after I finished my training in Italy as a conservator. That is what I do, I try my best to save old things from turning into dust and be forgotten. Sometimes there are beautiful things to save in beautiful places, if you are lucky. Sometimes, if you are incredibly lucky, you are even working with beautiful people on a daily basis. It is a rare event, but it can happen. And that is exactly what happened to me when I came to Duart.

I started working at Duart on the 27th of March 2016. It was a lovely Scottish spring day, as you can imagine. Pouring buckets of rain one minute and then sunshine the other. Then it was hailstones. You know the drill if you have been living in Scotland long enough.

I was involved in the Duart Restoration Project as part of the team that, at the time, was in charge of the restoration of the woodwork within the castle. During this phase, the castle was still not completely waterproof, so the main task was to improve water tightness of roof sections and windows. Our job was mainly focused on restoring the 1910s windows and improve their functionality. It was not an easy task as you can imagine if you know a bit about Duart and its location. A stronghold that withstands Scottish winter weather from the Atlantic and torrential rains for most of the year. A nightmare from a preservation point of view, but a dream that comes true as a professional and human experience.

Again, I was lucky to work on a project of this scale, not just for the stunning location and the historic importance of the site, but for the challenge we have been facing and the people we have been working with in the last five years. Most importantly for what you can learn from them.

Everybody at Duart is tough. You have to be tough if you want to survive winter and then enjoy the rest of the year. I do not mean only physically though, as you can imagine how hard it might be to be working on a Scottish castle in winter, outdoors, in 60 mph winds. I mean mentally tough.

Starting from Andy, the main contractor at Duart. As a stonemason with 40 plus years of experience, you can already imagine how strong the man might be, especially if you look at his hands. Massive hands. But what really impresses me about Andy it is not his strength, but his resolution. He is like a well-made diesel engine; he never gives up. Day in, day out. Even after the accident he had at the castle, where he seriously risked his life, he did not give up on Duart. I will never thank him enough for the opportunity to be part of his team of craftsmen, it has been a great master to learn from about Scottish heritage, skills, traditional techniques, and different approaches in the conservation world and in life.

You should know that approach is everything at Duart, and not just professionally.

As I said we are lucky to be part of a professional team, especially when overseen by Martin Hadlington, the main architect in charge of the restoration project at Duart. Martin has a big responsibility in guiding us during the process and guaranteeing that the right approach is tailored around the building. Martin's strength is his passion and commitment to this project, he really eats, drinks and breaths Duart. He would spend countless hours looking at the details within the building, losing himself on a small detail out of some carvings, or trying to match the 1910s restoration architect Burnet's drawings to the existing decorations. From him I learned how passionate you can be about what you do for a living.

But the toughest of them all is the Chief. Sir Lachlan Maclean. Sir Lachlan is a true son of Duart, tough but just. You can really see that in his eyes. He is as tough as the building can be, but being a man, it is not an easy task. Sir Lachlan is the way he is because he has to be. It is his duty for preserving his family heritage. For carrying the weight of a gigantic restoration project on his shoulders for years. For living on a building site that is also his home, his family home.

This overwhelming pressure must sometimes get to him, most people do not know him well enough to understand what this man has seen and what he has been through, especially at Duart. Some days are better than others and when he is in the mood I really like to laugh at his jokes, that I really find very close to my 'not-very-British' sense of humour. From him I have learned what real commitment is, that sometimes you cannot give up, as you have no choice.

Last but not least, the 'Guardians of Duart', as I call them, Alison and Ray. They really are beautiful people, and it is always nice to spend a word with them. They always have kind words for you and really make you feel like you are at home, even if you are in the middle of nowhere in the middle of a storm in the middle of a pandemic.

I spent some months of the lockdown at Duart with all these people and I would say that if it was not for the way they are and how they deal with life it might have been much worse. As you can imagine all your feelings are amplified during lockdown but, at the end of the day, all you need to go on is just a 'thank you', a smile, appreciation for what you do. The rain does not matter, the wind, working away solo, social distancing. As long as you've got that, you can do it. You know you have a purpose and that gets you thorough it, even if lockdown measures are tough, you cannot see your family back in Italy, you cannot go to a funeral, you cannot meet with your friends. If you have a purpose, you can do it. If you are passionate about it, even better. If you are committed, you cannot fail.

When I was not working at Duart I was lucky enough to work in my workshop, working away. I was also able to work a bit on the house and spend some time with my partner, playing my piano, cooking some proper meals as you have the time to do it, work in the garden. That I am glad for.

Sometimes I still think of those tough times when it was really hard to keep going, then I think of Andy, I think of Martin, Sir Lachlan, Ray and Alison. The way they approach life at Duart, and they keep going.

As Andy sometimes tells me: 'If it was easy Jonny, everybody would do it!' He has a point

25 - AUGUST 2020

The Scottish Government announce that COVID-19 remains a significant threat to public health and introduces new regulations for the hospitality industry. It becomes mandatory for hospitality settings to collect the contact details of visitors to their premises in support of Test and Protect.

The biggest change that we had made to the visitor experience in the castle was to shift the entrance so that visitors walked around the courtyard and in what had previously been the exit. This meant that the guide who was stationed inside could make sure that no one could enter without their details being taken for Scotland's Test & Protect scheme. They were also introduced to our safety protocols.

In the beginning this was not exactly succinct. I subjected early visitors to a long, scripted presentation that covered almost every Covid related modification we had made in excruciating detail. To add to their misery as this induction went on for so long, I sometimes forgot where I had got to and had to start over. I could watch people's beards grow while they waited patiently for me to stutter to a halt.

If early 2020 visitors were foolish enough to ask me a question about the castle's history, they soon wished they had packed a picnic and maybe a sleeping bag, so starved was I of company. Sometimes I would turn to point out some arcane point of interest and on turning back find a blank space where my audience had been standing 30 seconds before.

Part of my spiel was about our traffic light signs that warned people of potential 'pinch points' and I started to rue the fact that the Chief's predecessors had been rather negligent in failing to foresee a pandemic, because one day they might need to use a yellow tartan as part of the traffic light warning system. It already included the red and green of the Maclean of Duart tartans, so we decided that we needed a yellow one.

Not an official Maclean tartan, but one that would serve a purpose for the duration of the extra safety measure. Who better to design a new tartan than some of the younger residents of the island? With that in mind the Chief wrote to the head teachers of all seven primary schools on Mull and Iona, inviting them to design a yellow based tartan that we could use. All we had to do was sit back and wait.

We had deferred opening the tearoom until we were confident that we could comply with the appropriate guidelines and had sufficient visitors to make it worthwhile. After a couple of weeks of steady but not dramatic visitor numbers we took the decision to open on a limited take-away only basis.

This meant that Fiona could work without the need for extra staff. The usual tearoom seating area would remain as the waiting area for the shop and tearoom, necessary with Mull's unpredictable weather and when the shop could only accommodate two people at a time to maintain social distancing.

With the castle, shop and tearoom open we felt like we were returning to normality, or at least some form of it. We had positive feedback from visitors that our arrangements were reassuring but did not intrude on their enjoyment of Duart.

Fiona and Arianna worked hard to provide the best possible service that they could under the restrictions we had to work with. We did get a couple of negative comments about the restaurant not being open, but the rules for providing sit down meals, even just somewhere to perch inside while enjoying a cuppa, meant we would need at least two more staff members and could only seat around half of our usual number of diners. Visitor numbers just didn't justify the increased cost.

It was hard, for us, the visitors, and the business but generally we felt it worked and the overwhelming feedback was encouraging. Like all reviews you dwell on the one in a hundred that is not so positive.

Just a gentle note here that if your review of this book isn't glowing, I'll pop round and duff you up.[6]

Perhaps the most commented upon member of staff was the Chief. He was head groundskeeper, out in all weathers emptying the bins and litter picking, often before the rest of us were even awake. After lunch he usually mowed the lawns or weeded the paths. In his floppy sunhat and ancient, fraying jumper he would be as likely to be greeting visitors

---

[6] Not really.

and offering advice on good walks in the area as he was snipping the grass with edging shears or sorting out the recycling.

He also collected up and sorted the days takings from all parts of the business, project managed the restoration and I suspect spent his spare time studying the art of Uno from the original manuscripts of ancient masters.

On August 14th it became mandatory for hospitality settings to collect the contact details of visitors to their premises in support of Test and Protect. We'd been doing it since we opened a month before, so we were able to be unbearably smug for a little while.

My aura of smugness did not last long. Less than an hour in fact. I had already tried to drink coffee through my mask, misplaced, found, and then lost again a set of keys, and stepped in something unpleasant that an apparently rather ill and incontinent deer had left behind.

Now, in a foolish attempt to step over the ornamental chain around the courtyard my shoe became inexplicably attracted to it and I ended up performing a one-legged press-up in my best suit, to the amusement of the group I was supposed to be introducing to the castle.

In fairness they did show concern, or maybe pity, and after my less that glamourous start the rest of my speech seemed to pass without incident.

Courtyard introductions are always interesting, hopefully for the visitors, but also for the guide. We try and gauge a group's appetite for Duart history and shape our introduction accordingly. Children tend to get restless unless we include some of the castle's bloodier history, and some folk on bus tours have already seen 12 castles, 3 cathedrals, 22 lochs and visited 97 tearooms before they get to us, so it's our job to make Duart stand out as the special place that it is.

Occasionally though, you get that one person who steadfastly refuses to enjoy themselves. They will stand stock still with arms folded and a determined, 'go on then, let's get this over with' look on their face. That isn't usually a problem because for every one of them, there are the smilers, the gigglers, the head nodders, note takers (always slightly intimidating) the wise questioners and of course the enthusiastic Macleans.

But somehow one's eye is always drawn to the one person who put their grumpy pants on that morning and refuses to change them.

I recounted the history, added a couple of jokes, frightened the children with bloodthirsty deeds and overall, felt it had gone well. Finally, I explained that all visitors, unless exempt on medical grounds, had to wear a suitable face covering while inside the building. It was at this point that Mr Grumpy Pants surpassed himself as he ceremoniously put on his mask ... with a downturned frowning mouth on it.

Perfect I thought, at least he is consistent.

Most people are already wearing their masks when they come in and to the casual observer it could appear that the guide is being held up by a gang of wild west outlaws. Some of the masks can be quite intimidating too. We have faced printed skulls, open jaws with bloody fangs, something suspiciously like a WW2 gas mask and a four-year-old wearing a full dragon costume including face mask to match.

We have seen them all, from the dust filters Dad bought from the DIY store 10 years ago and found at the bottom of his toolkit, to bejewelled and colour coordinated fashion statements, and all points in-between.

To our utmost delight though no one refused to wear one or caused us a problem. One or two may not have been happy about it, but no one sought to argue with us.

Before I leave the area of Castle introductions, a word of acknowledgement to Martyn and Nic who taught me the ropes, although evidently not the chain, and without whom I'd still be floundering.

Towards the end of August, I decided to pop into the castle to touch up some paint that had been niggling me. I appeared in my de-fault workman outfit. Special tough trousers with 12 pockets of varying shapes and sizes, knee pads, nylon loops for goodness knows what, a carabiner, my old Tottenham Hotspur FC sweatshirt and heavy boots that may once have been light brown.

'Are you sure about this?' Asked my lovely wife, taking a step back in case the brush I was holding was wet.

'Yup, it'll only take a few minutes…'

Two and a half hours later I popped back for a coffee.

'How much have you done?' Asked my beloved, while gently ushering me onto newspaper.

'Just the bit where the poster was changed and pulled the paint off.'

Alison looked at her watch. Then at the clock in

case her watch was wrong.

'The tiny patch in the Sea Room?'

I could see where this was going. But I was a self-appointed master craftsman and not to be outmanoeuvred...

'Yes, but I had to prepare it, sand it down, sharpen my brushes and...'

I withered under her look of bewildered pity.

'I'm sure you've done a good job' she said kindly, or patronisingly, depending on your point of view... 'but darling, how did you get so much paint on yourself?'

Looking down I could see her point. My trousers and shirt, and it turned out my face and somehow inside my left sock, were a little 'painty'.

'I really don't know. I don't think paint likes me.'

'I don't know... it seems quite attracted to you...'

Earlier in the year I had a few painting jobs to do and when I bumped into Jonny, who does this sort of thing professionally and, I cannot help noticing, without turning himself into a human canvas, he thought I had spilled the paint.

'No, just a few splashes' I said, and hurried off. I'd have waved goodbye, but the paint on my sleeve was beginning to dry and further movement wouldn't be possible if I was delayed.

Other than my usual calamitous approach to DIY, the season was shaping up well.

The shop was being steered through the storm admirably with Anne at the helm. Sales were down, but steady, and were being partly offset by an increase in internet orders. The tearoom continued to do takeaways, which Fiona or Arianna prepared and served by themselves, and when sunny weather brought the crowds out, they were whirling around like dervishes.

One other thing that we noticed was that we had been able to meet and greet every single visitor, a luxury that we would not normally have enjoyed. That added personal touch is one of the plus points from a lean season.

August 2020

Dry days 13,
Max temperature 27.6,
Min temperature 6.9,
Max wind speed 36.9 mph,
Monthly rainfall 5.54 mm.

Visitor numbers compared to August 2019 - down 71%.

26 – ROYAL CONNECTIONS

Before it was decommissioned in 1997 and turned into a tourist attraction Her Majesty's Yacht (HMY) Britannia was a regular sight from the battlements of Duart. Some local people recall being invited to the castle to wave white bedsheets as she sailed past.

Sometimes, thanks to the Chief's father's position as Lord Chamberlain to the Queen, the Royal family would sail past on their way to their holiday at Balmoral. The Chief remembers how, as a teenager he was dispatched by his father to fetch the Queen and Prince Philip and row them to the slipway.

He recalls his feelings of awe and terror at being charged with this duty and trying not to bump or splash the Royal party while ferrying them ashore.

HMY Britannia sailed past Duart on her final voyage in 1997 and exchanged salutes (blanks fired from cannon) with Duart. Pictures of the event are on display in the castle.

Incidentally, one of the regular small cruise ships to bring visitors to Duart is the MV Hebridean Princess, which has been chartered by Her Majesty the Queen on two occasions since the decommissioning of HMY Britannia, for holidays afloat around Scotland.

27 – CAROL WAGEMAKERS

'I am instantly removed of any worries and enter this oasis of peace and tranquillity.'

Duart Castle has a small walled garden, that is a private space for the Chief and his family. About 10 years ago Lady Rosemary had what was once a disused cattle yard made into a garden.

My name is Carol Wagemakers and I am the Castle gardener.

On arriving for work and opening the door that leads into the garden, I am instantly removed of any worries and enter this oasis of peace and tranquillity, with a light step and a smile in my face that has been so essential during this pandemic year.

Working with nature in the outdoors is very calming, well most of the time! The blood pressure rises on occasions, when on entering the glass house, I see that the slugs have been out for a temperance party. They have ignored the beer traps and gorged on seedlings!

Gardening is never a lonely occupation, there is almost always the ubiquitous Robin, *Erithacus Rubecula*, patiently waiting for his worm feast as the soil is turned over or picking at the sand-hoppers, *Talitrus Saltator,* that will be leaping amongst the tangle of mixed seaweeds that has been applied as a garden mulch.

This very week of writing, I looked up to the sound of 30 Whooper Swans, *Cygnus Cygnus*, flying north over the garden to their Tundra breeding grounds of Iceland.

The garden is divided into 4 sections. Soft fruit and shrubs, raised beds for vegetables, ornamental beds and polytunnel. The vegetables will be used by the Chief and his family, while the polytunnel grows salad leaves, tomatoes and cucumbers for the tearoom. This year strawberries are growing in there in hanging baskets to keep the slugs away from the fruit.

Each area is surrounded by Yew hedging *Taxus Baccata*. I am a passionate gardener, and that leads me into wanting to explore the relationship between plants, their uses and people.

The yew, in history, has been used to make longbows, and archaeological study tells us that as far back as Neolithic time, people were using yew-wood bows. Clan badges often have a plant association, and the Fraser clan has the yew. Bagpipes were originally made from yew.

Looking around the garden spring is beginning to show itself; the snowdrops have finished and the daffodils are now in flower. They always bring a very happy smile at this time of year, but they are not just for picking. Both bulbs contain an alkaloid called

Galantamine which is used in the treatment of Alzheimers disease. Bluebells, *Endymian Non-scriptus*, are just beginning to put their linear leaves above ground. In times past the bluebell has been used as a glue, the sticky secreta from the stem, in book binding and a source of laundry starch. Again, a plant that has been used to aid Mankind.

The Elder, *Sambucas Nigra*, has just been pruned, which has a wealth of folklore attached to it. Farmers would whip their crops with leaves from elder, believing that they would be kept safe from blight. Milk was put under the tree to stop it from curdling and baked cakes were left underneath to keep safe from fairies!

The garden roses have also been pruned, and in history Bonnie Prince Charlie is said to have picked a wayside rose, believed to of been a Burnet rose, *Rosa Pimpinellifolia* – and pinned it to his bonnet as he marched Eastwards in 1745. The white rose is now seen as a symbol of nationalism by many in Scotland.

Rose hips are used in wine making and a rich vitamin C syrup.

From around the 14th century there were a family of physicians called Beaton. They were doctors to the Lords of the Isles on Islay and then spread out to other Scottish Islands on the West Coast. Beatons came to Mull in the late 1500s and there is a memorial cross to the family at Pennycross on the Ross of Mull.

The Beatons were physicians to the Macleans of Duart, and there were various herb gardens on Mull growing the necessary herbs. Plants were also collected from the wild and cliff and shore. These would have been made into tonics, ointments and other forms of medication.

One of the plants that the Beatons used, which grows in abundance in the wet boggy areas of the West Coast, is Bog Myrtle, *Myrica Gale*. It was used as a stimulant and other uses included making candles from wax in the leaves and twigs. The plant has legendary insect repelling properties and it is grown and harvested today as a repellent. Added to heather it has been used in beer making and the leaves can improve the foaming of beer. Recently it has been used as a botanic in gin making.

Another popular Beaton herb is Meadowsweet, *Filipendula Ulmaria*. This was used in the treatment of headaches, as a painkiller, and for the ease of stomach acid. The sweet smell of the flowers made it a popular strewing herb, and today is often used in cordials and flavouring ice-cream.

Honey suckle *Lonicera Periclymenum*, flowers were used in a syrup for asthma and an infusion of leaves was used as a laxative. Greater Plantain, *Plantago Major*, was used by the Beatons for healing wounds. Saxons used the herb bound to the head with red wool to cure headaches. Tea made from the leaves can help relieve throat infections.

So many plants and bark of trees were used by the physicians as herbal remedies. On reading this please do not try to make any of these remedies, whether they worked or did harm, I do not know.

The relationship between plants and people is a long and continuous one. Almost every plant in history has had a use of some kind, be it for food and drink, medicine, house building, thatching, textiles (nettle fabric has been found in Bronze Age burial sites), soaps, furniture and more. People have often referred to some of these plants as weeds, but it is these weeds that have been a basis of survival for most of human history.

28 -SEPTEMBER 2020

The Scottish economy shrunk by 19.4% during the second quarter of 2020, new restrictions are introduced for household visits and a national curfew for pubs, bars and restaurants come into force. Weekly cases on the continent are now higher than at the first peak of the disease in March and Covid-19 hospital admissions doubled in England over a fortnight.

August had passed with a steady increase in the number of visitors, including the very occasional bus tour. The buses gave us an opportunity to experience a busy castle again. We developed the technique of delivering the introduction on the bus, then admitting people in groups of six for a short safety talk. As soon as they had finished and started their tour, we admitted the next six for their talk, and so on. It worked well and it was the method that we adopted for the few bus tours that we had.

The bus tour guides were grateful and could not have been more understanding. The patrons were a delight and pleased to be anywhere that would have them during these strange times. They had disposable income, time, a keen interest in the castle, and more often than not reading glasses that fogged up the second they stepped inside.

I learned to use a visor with them because, well frankly because some of the clientele on the bus tours were of an age where they were subconsciously relying upon lip reading to help them. Visors were fine apart from the occasion when I boarded the bus wearing my mask, put the visor on, tried to take off my mask which snagged because I now had the elastic holding it in place threatening to snap my ears off. I removed the visor, whereby my mask pinged down the bus and into seat 7D. Luckily no one was decapitated by its flight down the bus. Imagine the insurance form for that!

One of the things we started showing off to people were freshly printed traffic light signs with a bright new yellow tartan courtesy of competition winner, 9-year-old Mia Lopes.

The competition received over 150 entries and the Chief chose the eventual winner, announcing in a press release:

'We want people to feel safe and looked after when they visit, so we came up with something that was memorable, could be understood easily by everyone and was a little quirky, but unfortunately none of my ancestors had thought to introduce a yellow based tartan, so I was delighted to receive so many entries and the standard was incredibly high.

I'm delighted that Mia Lopes from Tobermory Primary school has designed the winning entry and her design is being used in our new signs.

It was a very tough decision with so many great designs to choose from. The pupils of the islands' schools have much to be proud of and I'm pleased that so many took the time to help us here at Duart. I also extend my thanks to the teachers and staff who have had to face so many new challenges with the reopening of the schools.'

Later Mia and her family came to the castle for a presentation of her prize by the Chief. I took their picture on the steps, looking rather awkward as everyone tried to get in shot while remaining socially distant.

September included a few days when we struggled because of high numbers of people coming in. Normally it isn't a problem and this year we wanted to welcome them with open arms, but inclement weather, bored holiday makers and being the only indoor attraction open on Mull coincided to make us popular at a time when we should be limiting numbers.

Fiona was in the ticket hut and tried staggering people entering, but as there was no refuge outside, the Sea Room in the castle became a sort of soggy waiting room. I distracted guests by stretching out my introduction to ridiculous lengths until the next room became less crowded.

Patience was occasionally frayed, more due to the weather than us, but generally everyone understood. One rather well-spoken gentleman, the sort who favoured mustard coloured corduroy and gout, demanded to know why we had let his group in if we were so busy.

'We thought you'd like to wait inside' I replied, which his companions heartily agreed with.

'Humph, I think it's a bit crowded...'

I had to concur on this point and was mentally trying to find a way to suggest that he could wait outside in the rain if he wanted to, when a lady I assume was his wife intervened.

'I think it's fine Geoffrey[7], we'd all much rather wait in here than outside in the pouring rain.' She smiled the smile of the long-suffering spouse.

He begrudgingly agreed and proceeded to quiz me on our procedures while the rest of his party saw an opportunity to scurry off and enjoy the sights without him.

It wasn't just the castle that got busy on these wet days. The shop and tearoom were too. Anne darted around to help the tearoom out when she could and when Arianna was in, I would go into the ticket hut so that Fiona could help her out during our busiest times. This meant that we could bring on the castle guide super-sub for an hour or so...

The Chief.

Now, in fairness, he does know his stuff. He should do, it's his home and he is immersed in its history. Sometimes people paused on their way out and asked me who the gentleman showing them around was. In one case someone stopped to say it was incredibly good of the gardener to help out.

Reaction to being told he was the Chief and he lived in the castle was positive, but it did raise queries. One family refused to believe that anyone lived on site. Point blank denied it could be so, and thought I was pulling their leg.

---

[7] Not his real name, which was Bernard.

They started to get a bit cross that I kept insisting it was true. One of them pointed to the detached cottage and asked if he (the Chief) lived in it.

'No, that's reserved for the builders working here.'

'Oh, so he lives there' he said, pointing out the cottage where Alison and I reside.

'No, that's where I live.'

'But you're not from these parts…'

'I found the commute from Essex a bit of a strain…' (For those not familiar with the geography of the UK it's about 500 miles each away.)

'So, you live here now?'

'That is correct sir.'

'So, you are the Chief then?'

I knew when to give up.

After lunch Fiona returned and I went back into the castle. This meant locating my lunchtime replacement. Experience had taught me that he could be anywhere. I found the best way to find him was to follow the trail he left…radio in the Sea Room, ball point pen on the floor, reading glasses on the Banqueting Hall table… and so on until I found him talking to someone. He would then introduce me as the Chief and slink off with a mischievous twinkle in his eye.

One thing he refused to do was go into the ticket hut, on account of our till. We have swish computerised tills that can do all sorts of fancy things except make coffee and be straightforward to understand. When we got them, I foolishly offered to write a simple guide to using them. My first draft was longer than this book.

The ticket hut, guide and shop stay in touch with

each other during the working day by 2-way radio. It's useful when Anne needs extra change, or we can alert the tearoom to the imminent arrival of a bus group, or of course alert each other to the whereabouts of the Chief.

Not that anyone would ever be doing anything they should not be doing you understand! He does though have the uncanny ability to appear without any warning. Maybe it is his army training, but he could bounce on a pogo stick over bubble wrap while carrying dynamite without a single pop.

In the castle his stealth can be terrifying. Alison tells the tale of polishing the brass, merrily away somewhere warm and sunny in her mind, when she turned around and he was standing there like an apparition; and incredibly lucky not to be wearing 2 litres of brass polish.

Back at the cottage we had a hastily arranged visit from Alison's older brother and his family. They were taking advantage of a window in the pandemic restrictions and suddenly two extra adults, two grown-up boys and a 5-year-old girl were filling every nook and cranny of the cottage. It was a wonderful treat for us, and hopefully for them too.

When they arrived, having sped to Oban from Cambridge in record time, the car door opened, and every type of waterproof covering known to humankind sprung from within. Thanks to Alison's diligent preparations they arrived with wellington boots, at least two impermeable coats each, rain hats, gloves and scarfs, not unreasonably anticipating wall to wall wind and rain.

It was of course unbroken sunshine while they

stayed.

Somewhat embarrassingly we had run out of bottled gas two hours before they turned up, so the first meal was microwaved in batches. Then one of the toilets broke and I spent a jolly evening muttering to myself and waving tools around. The lavatory refused to listen to reason or to be intimidated by my threats, so I had to fix it.

I hate plumbing. I consider it like gardening and embalming, you can either do it, or you are normal.

It was eventually repaired with the assistance of Alison's sister-in-law, a new gas bottle arrived, and we spent four wonderful days getting cooked under the relentless sun. Wine and whisky were drunk, bread was broken, laughter filled the air, songs were sung, although not by me because I have the singing voice of a welk, and we even went swimming in the sea.

Three weeks after their visit a couple stood at the ticket hut with rain dripping from their inappropriate summer clothes. He was distinctly unimpressed and kept looking at me oddly, I realised that he was trying to read my name badge, so I pointed my left breast at him provocatively and away they squelched.

Alison was inside guiding and when she had finished her introduction the same couple approached, and he declared that he had a bone to pick with her. Normally this is not the precursor to a cheerful conversation, but it turned out they were friends of Alison's brother who had been assured by him that the weather on Mull was glorious and that they should pack extra shorts and a sun hat.

They all had a good chuckle and after exchanging stories about her brother that both parties can use in evidence should the need arise, they went to have a good look around the castle and left Alison to mop up the floor where they had been standing.

September 2020

Dry days 11,
Max temperature 25.1,
Min temperature 2.8,
Max wind speed 29.5 mph,
Monthly rainfall 9.28 mm.

Visitor numbers compared to September 2019 – down 79%.

29 - MORE FILM CONNECTIONS

Episode 9 of the third season of Game of Thrones features *'The Red Wedding'*, a massacre at a wedding ceremony. George R.R. Martin, author of the A Song of Ice and Fire novels, on which the series is based, sites two sources from Scottish history as his inspiration. The Black Dinner of 1440 that features in Clan Douglas history, when two children were given a 'mock' trial, found guilty of high treason, and beheaded. His other source was the Glencoe Massacre of 1691, when soldiers murdered 38 people, after accepting hospitality from them.

In the 1975 film Monty Python and the Holy Grail, Sir Lancelot, played by John Cleese, causes bloody mayhem at a wedding on his way to rescue a princess, who turns out to be a prince.

Duart Castle can claim its own wedding story that is arguably closer to the Game of Thrones version than the sources credited, and it isn't dissimilar to the Monty Python scene filmed at Doune Castle on the Scottish mainland. The 14th Chief, another Sir

Lachlan, raided the wedding of his widowed mother, murdered eighteen of the wedding guests and imprisoned the groom-to-be and according to the castle records made him suffer 'dailie tortour and pains'.

30 - BEHZAD REZA-ZADEH

'Learning the difference between yes and no cost me six teeth...'

Anyone visiting Duart while the building work has been going on cannot help but notice a cheery face beaming out from somewhere between a dayglo high visibility jacket and a safety helmet. Often the rest of his face is obscured by a dust mask and googles too, but the smile always breaks through.

Behzad is a part of the Duart story now. Such is his dedication that he spent Christmas 2020 working on site. He resisted attempts to lure him with food and drink, until Alison finally convinced him to join Anne and myself in the cottage after he had finished working.

Under polite questioning his story emerged and if I had not been under the influence of a rather nice sherry or three, I would have grabbed my notebook there and then. He did though agree to be interviewed for this book, so one chilly February evening we sat down together.

Could you tell us a little about your background?

My family are from the city of Shiraz in Southern Iran. It's a beautiful place with numerous gardens and a lot of history. There are many fine old buildings.

I am the youngest of 7 brothers and I also have 2 sisters, one younger than me. We were quite poor growing up, so I left school at 13 years old and went to work. My family are all builders, and I learnt my trade and to build houses.

I had my own business and built many houses that we rented out. I was proud of everything I had achieved.

Then you came to England?

Yes. I had to escape from Iran when I was 27 years old. I came here as a refugee.

So, you had to leave your family behind, and you ended up in England?

Yes, I had to flee quickly.

I lived in a hostel for a while, then I was sent to Sheffield. I had no English and learned what I could as I went along. For example, I used to get confused because I would see 'To Let' signs and look for the toilet.

I was helped by a family through a local church. The man was a judge and they taught me basic English. I was not allowed to work until I received my permission to stay in the UK. That was difficult because I wanted a job.

Then I was given leave to remain in the UK and

got permission to work.

I thought to myself… It is possible to live in Sheffield and speak Farsi, my native language because there are a lot of Iranians there, but I had to learn English and I must find work. A lot of people helped me, but I had to find myself, find my own way.

So, I caught the train to Glasgow and found somewhere to live.

Were you able to speak English by then?

No. I refused an interpreter because I knew I must learn to speak it. When I was in Glasgow, I had toothache, so I went to a dentist and he removed several teeth before finding the right one. It cost me 6 teeth to learn the difference between Yes and No!

That must have been a painful lesson.

It was, but I soon learned. I started work in a Persian restaurant and went to college to learn English. First year was part time, then two years full time.

That was where I met my 'Greek Mum'. A lovely lady also studying English, who really helped me and introduced me to my girlfriend, who was at college there too.

So, how did you end up working at Duart Castle?

I started again as a builder and was working with Jonny. He taught me to restore windows and brought me along to Duart to help. He and Andy have taught me a lot, because I needed to know the correct words for all the tools and materials you need as a builder.

I started to learn about the Castle.

You obviously like the castle…
It is beautiful. I love finding out about its history and discovering things. I feel like the stones breathe and could tell stories. I like seeing new things too, like the little shells in the mortar where the old builders used sand from the beach. I get extremely excited when I'm coming back here and see it.

How did you feel when the castle went into lockdown?
At first, I had a rest, but I like to work. I got incredibly sad not being able to work. I had too much time to think about my family and Shiraz. If I'm not at Duart I try and work at weekends, it stops me thinking about what I left behind in Iran.

With work I ache physically. If I am not working, I ache in my heart.

That must be hard for you. I understand that you cannot go back to Iran?
Not legally, no. Sometimes I get sad and depressed about it. But I must carry on and make my new life here. I like to work and keep busy, plus the internet means that I can stay in touch with my family, but I cannot hold them.

When you are not at work, what do you do to relax?
I like to exercise. I have an exercise bike and weights. I like to cycle too. One of my brothers was a very good cyclist and coached a team in Iran. I'm looking forward to being able to cycle around Mull,

when the weather is a little warmer.

What does the future hold for you Behzad?

I want to buy and restore an old house, maybe not a castle like Duart, but something old where I can put what I have learned to good use.

My ambition is to buy a motorbike and travel around the world. I want to experience different languages; eat local food and I want to see the Great Wall of China. I want to see how it was built!

I have to keep going forward.

Behzad shared with me his reasons for leaving Iran, which we have chosen to keep private. Suffice to say one does not choose to leave your whole family, the place you love and everything that you have achieved without good cause.

31 – OCTOBER 2020

The Scottish Government announce new measures, restricting indoor hospitality opening, and severely limiting the sale of alcohol. Outdoor live events, adult contact sports and indoor group exercise classes are stopped, and some recreation premises have to shut. Shops across Scotland returns to two metre physical distancing and reintroduce many of the restrictions they put in place earlier in the pandemic.

The pandemic seemed to be ramping up again. Although the season was significantly shorter than usual and the working day not as long, we were all exhausted. Andrew Maclean had gone home in case work summoned him, Jonny popped in occasionally to swap windows over for renovation, and otherwise spent most of his time at his workshop on the mainland. Behzad was as busy as ever and Andy was conducting the restoration armed with a jack hammer only slightly smaller than himself.

We had decided to stay open for one week longer than usual in October to catch the last of the sunseekers who would be flocking to Mull for the Autumn half term.

As it turned out October was – quiet.

Very quiet.

In the hut my mind wandered. Occasionally it would take itself on vacation without permission and was very reluctant to return. I made notes for a book, talked to the occasional visitor until they feigned death to get away, talked to a crow I christened Eric, played with my phone until I accidentally called a stranger in Mexico, talked to myself and drank coffee.

Coffee – the most cherished of the warm beverage family. Strong and black. No sugar, no fancy frothy nonsense, no added flavours or ridiculous infusions, no milk or cream. Just pure coffee. The first coffee of the day is something to treasure, as is the second and third. The fourths not too shabby either.

The Chief would often intercept Alison or me carrying coffee to the hut, it was another of his uncanny stealth mode activities. One day in October he stepped out from behind a tree just as Alison, who is prone to jumpiness (she lives with me after all) was walking by with two steaming mugs. It was fortunate that she was wearing her mackintosh, I remarked as she handed me half a cup of stone-cold coffee. It's not just the coffee that gives her the jitters, its sly Highland Chieftains too.

The downside of drinking coffee, particularly for a gentleman of my middling years, is the urge to unload it. When I was young, I was impressed by things like jet planes, knights in armour and how many Fruit Pastels I could fit in my mouth. Today I'm genuinely astonished by going from 10am to 1pm without needing a wee. Alone in the ticket hut is not the ideal place to be caught short. An ex-castle guide tells of the time he could not raise his colleague on the radio and had to resort to an empty water bottle and hope no one chose that time to approach the hut.

Suffice to say I usually managed to get through until lunchtime. That's all I'm going to say on the matter.

Suddenly that was it. The seasons was at an end.

The day after we closed the doors on the final day, we were all busy with packing up and other fun diversions. The tearoom takes some time and after the necessary minimum Fiona took the opportunity for a weekend off before returning to dive into the clearing, cleaning, stocktaking, and storing everything away.

Anne started to pack the shop away. This is always a painstaking task, particularly for the stock that will be sold on-line, because it must be accessible and carefully stored, labelled by size and/or colour and be ready to be grabbed and packaged up when an order comes in. And not, and this was made quite clear to me the one year I tried to lend a hand, shoved into the cupboard willy-nilly with no record of the stock numbers.

I don't know, you try and help.

Carol was busy doing whatever dark rituals gardeners do to appease the spirit of winter and ensure the next growing season to be bountiful. I think she sacrifices slugs on an altar of red cabbage. I've caught her chanting before, she swore that she was just singing along to her personal stereo, but I'm not convinced.

I was kept occupied loading the outdoor furniture away. This, as we discovered in February was a job that demanded careful stacking. Fortunately, I found that my time at the Jenga tables of Casino Duart during the spring was not wasted, and they fitted together perfectly in an indomitable tower of lumber.

At the tail end of October, we had the opportunity to spend some time with Alison's son and his girlfriend. Back in August, furloughed from work and assured that he would not be required for some time, they went to visit her family in Poland. All well and good - until it wasn't.

Poland went into lockdown, flights home were severely limited and they became stranded. In the end they flew back to Scotland and went into quarantine with us during October. We had to be extra careful as we had two potential Covidites living with us.

A fortnight later all of us were declared hunky dory so they were free to wander the streets of Mull. Despite their usual urban habitat, they became wildlife talisman. In their company we saw Golden and White Tailed (sea) Eagles, Red and Roe Deer, Seals, Otters, Barn Owls and all sorts of other critters.

Alison's son may usually live in London, but he has lived in slightly more rural parts, whereas his girlfriend is a city dweller through and through. I think Mull was a bit of a shock to her, but she did fall in love with a trio of young ginger highland coos down the road from us. She christened them Bobby, Martin and Nelson.

We didn't have the heart to tell her they were all females.

After two extra weeks, while they negotiated a new

tenancy in London, we drove them to Glasgow and dropped them off for their train south. It wasn't quite a case of slowing down and tipping them out, but it was a quick drop off and departure. We wanted to minimise contact with anyone else so that we could integrate back into Mull without undue quarantining.

It had been a month of mixed emotions, it brought everyone closer, and for two young city people stuck in a remote spot on an island, they coped admirably.

October 2020

Dry days 5,
Max temperature 18.6,
Min temperature 1.8,
Max wind speed 46.8 mph,
Monthly rainfall 5.31 mm.

Visitor numbers compared to October 2019 - down 64%.

32 – BLACK'S TOWER

Passing on the ferry from Oban to Mull you may see what looks like a small castle on the port, or left, side of the vessel, a little way before Duart. This is a lighthouse that was built in 1900 in a spot favoured by Glasgow born novelist William Black (1841-1898). It was commissioned by a group of his friends as a tribute to him. He trained as a landscape painter and later became a journalist and war correspondent before turning to writing full time when his novels started to become popular. Among his most renown books are: *'The Princess of Thule,' 'A Daughter of Heth,' and 'Macleod of Dare'*, which features a fictional castle that may sound familiar...

'...The smooth Atlantic swell was booming along the somber caves; but up here in Castle Dare, on the high and rocky coast of Mull, the great hall was lit with such a blaze of candles as Castle Dare had but rarely seen...'

William Black would only have known Duart as a ruin when he came to sit on the rocks overlooking the Sound of Mull and write. His description of the fictional castle closely resembles the layout of those ruins and he would undoubtably have known Duart well, even though most of the action set on Mull happens around the Ross area, where the author stayed.

The tower was commemorated by Lord Archibald Campbell, former President of the Highland Association, with this poem:

> *We fain would let thy memory dwell,*
> *Where rush the tideways of the sea,*
> *Where storms will moan or calms will tell,*
> *To all the world, our love for thee.*
> *Whom all men loved in this old land,*
> *And all men loved across the sea-*
> *We well may clasp our brethren's hand,*
> *And light the Beacon light for thee!*

Incidentally, Black is a recognised Sept of Clan Maclean, although I think in this case it's just coincidence that William chose Duart and its surroundings to write.

Blacks Tower offers a lovely short walk from Duart when the weather is reasonable, although caution should always be taken on slippery slopes. For anyone prepared for scrambling over rocks you can see the remains of the gas pipes and mooring rings nearby, left over from when it was gas powered and had to be regularly refuelled from a boat.

33 - ARIANNA PRETORIUS

'My seasonal road rage was greatly reduced this year.'

My name is Arianna Pretorius. I am originally from Peebles in the Scottish Borders. I moved to the Isle of Mull in July 2016, when my now husband took a job on the island. I started working at the Duart Tearoom in April 2017.

One of my favourite things about Duart is pulling up at the start of the working day and taking in the beautiful view of the castle and its surroundings, which changes every day.

As one of the few staff members who did not live on site, I drove back and forth from Tobermory each day. One of the best things about lockdown was that my seasonal road rage was greatly reduced. Fewer people on the roads driving at 5mph or blocking the passing places or road to take pictures of Highland coos.

The worst thing about lockdown for me, was not being able to visit friends and family. I missed my weekend trips back to the Borders greatly.

During Lockdown when I was unable to work, I tried to keep busy the best I could. I enjoyed baking and cooking, which was not always easy when the local supermarket did not get deliveries, or the shops freezers broke down yet again. Thankfully, my husband is not a fussy eater and we had a few random meals made up with whatever could be found in the bottom of the freezer and back of the kitchen cupboards.

When permitted to do so we spent a lot of time walking our dog Spencer around different parts of the island, including the grounds of Duart which remained open to the public. On one trip to the grounds, we spent almost an hour sitting on a rock below the castle watching a pod of dolphins.

34 – NOVEMBER 2020

Potential Covid-19 vaccines show up to 90% effectiveness. The Scottish Government announce new COVID-19 protection levels and new travel regulations, including restrictions on travelling outside of your local authority except for essential purposes. A UK-wide 'limited relaxation' of coronavirus restrictions between 23 and 27 December, with restrictions on numbers, is announced. In the US cases touch 200,000 a day before the end of the month.

At the end of October, Alison and I managed to get a break. We took Mavis our motorhome so that we could stay independent, plus we really missed driving around in her. Packed up and off the island we stopped overnight in Buxton, Derbyshire. This is an area of outstanding natural beauty that we know well, but we were not going to linger for long.

We were up bright and early the following morning...well, early anyway. Okay not early but we got up before noon and directed Mavis due south to alight at Alison's parents' house outside Cambridge as dusk settled.

We had all the awkward encounters one experiences when trying to be socially distant while being familial, and I suspect secret feminine hugs were exchanged while Alison's father and I were not looking. Still, it all went swimmingly and after a brief period of recuperation we continued south to the settlement of Worthing where my eldest and his fiancé had completed the purchase of their first home a couple of days before lockdown would have scuppered their plans.

While there we met my other son in London for a romp around the delights of Tottenham, North London. This was where my parents met, and I was finalising research for a book about them, so I dragged Alison and my boy around dreary places that even locals did not consider interesting. It was all very nostalgic, I made notes, took photos and we found a wonderful pub that served good beer, splendid pizza and accepted Scottish currency.[8]

All told we had a successful trip but cut it short as new, stricter restrictions were about to come into force in England and not wanting to fall foul of the law we drove north and stopped overnight just south of the Scottish border.

This should have been simple, after all we were driving around with an en-suite bedroom. However, we had stopped to gather up our remaining furniture and possessions from storage on the way home. This meant that Mavis was packed to the roof, and everything was held in place by sticky tape and luck.

---

[8] Currency issued by all countries of the UK is legal tender throughout the land but the further south one travels the harder it is to convince people that notes printed in Scotland are legitimate.

I was driving the last stretch and was warned to be careful because a sharp application of the brakes might well decapitate my beloved. A point she felt unnecessary to mention when she was driving, and I was apparently a mere excited press of a pedal away from a shelving unit removing my head.

Anyway, we arrived safely at the hotel, which was due to shut the following day because of the impending restrictions. After a comfy night and careful securing of the load behind the passenger seat in lieu of breakfast, we chugged our way home.

It was welcome break, and we were fortunate to get it. Much of the world was shut down. Anne was stuck in Scotland all winter and had not seen her family back in New Zealand for over nine months, and with little chance of seeing them anytime soon. People around the country, and the rest of the world, were in difficult circumstances and the news around this latest lockdown and associated restrictions wasn't likely to ease thing soon.

While we were away a miraculous event had occurred at the castle. It happens at the end of every season. Everything is packed away, stored securely, or otherwise covered, packed up or moved to a place of safety. The Chief's sister arrives every October and is the principal engineer behind the ritual disassembly of the exhibits.

The process is reversed in the spring when the exhibits are dusted down and put back with commendable accuracy. I have discovered her folded up inside display cases arranging exhibits with an almost military precision, draped in a white dust sheet (which is a scary encounter in a castle dungeon) and balancing on a chair with a feather duster in one hand, polish in the other and holding a screwdriver in her teeth.

In normal circumstances she would bring a friend or two to help but for obvious reasons this was not an ordinary year, so she and the Chief had been at work for the duration of our southern jaunt.

Also hard at work were Andy and Behzad, who were preparing the Sea Room for a winter makeover. Jonny had been in to reinstall some of the windows he had restored and taken had taken more away with him for renovation, and Fiona was finalising arrangements to leave.

Anne, Fiona, Alison and I are all keen walkers, although we've never teamed up, generally preferring hiking as a solo or couple's event. I must admit I enjoy a solo romp myself. The chance to commune with nature, lose myself in the privacy of my own head and pee against whatever tree I fancy really does wonders for the soul, although possibly not for the tree.

Today though Alison and I went to Carsaig. If you have never been there it is well worth the excursion. It is featured in the 1945 Powell and Pressburger film '*I Know Where I'm Going*', along with Duart Castle masquerading as the fictional Castle of Sorne.

Just the drive is worth the trip. Turning off the Craignure to Iona road at Pennyghael you drive along a narrow track which steadily, then suddenly, descends in a series of turns and switchbacks with glimpses of the sea and the island of Colonsay floating on the horizon. Colonsay doubled as the imaginary island of Kiloran in *I know Where I'm Going*.

The way becomes wooded and even more dramatic until halfway down the hill where you will find a bright red telephone box plumb next door to a raging waterfall. This makes calls difficult to hear, a situation exploited to humorous effect in a certain film that you are getting tired of me mentioning.

Eventually the road levels out at a small carpark in a snug spot behind an old boathouse and the remnants of Carsiag pier. The boathouse is worth a look, as it sports the engraved Coat of Arms of the Macleans of Pennycross.

You now have two choices. Right takes you, eventually, to Carsaig Arches. These are natural sea arches a fair distance away. I wrote about our almost disastrous walk to them in Still Following Rainbows.

Today we turned left to what was new territory new to us. There is a track that leads around the headland to Lochbuie, 8.5 kms away, although we would only be going part way today.

We took the track behind some holiday-let cottages and through scenic woodland on a gently undulating path that brought us out into a boggy pasture. A squelch and slurp or two later and we forded a burn and dropped into the sort of rough craggy path that we love.

Between the rock-strewn shoreline and the cliffs, we rambled like delighted toddlers. Up and down, around wonderful rock formations, gazing into rock pools, we stopped to admire the basalt columns high up on the cliffs. The same type of columns make up The Giants Causeway in Northern Ireland and closer to home, the foreboding cliffs of Staffa. Occasionally we'd discover pieces of these columns had broken away and some perfect hexagonal salmon pink rocks lay scattered about.

There were ominous caves in the cliffs, one or two of which we peeked into without any enthusiasm to go further in, until joy upon joy, we found a cave behind a waterfall! This meant that we could stand inside and look out to the rugged shoreline through cascading water. It was magical.

Soggy but exhilarated, we carried on to a point where the shoreline opened out onto a plateau of mossy pools and exposed rocks. There's an old sea stack here known as An Dun (The Fort), which has a cave with a bench and graffiti lined walls.

After a leisurely exploration we headed back the way we had come. We stopped and watched an eagle being driven away by hooded crows, saw a seal bob up and watch us pass, and then when we got back to the pier, we ate lunch while watching an otter swimming out in the shallows and bringing its prey back to eat. It was a magical day, Mull in miniature.

November 2020

Dry days 6,
Max temperature 15.4,
Min temperature 3.0,
Max wind speed 41.8 mph,
Monthly rainfall 16.34 mm.

35 - SURVEYS

Most people in the UK are familiar with Ordinance Survey maps. They are the standard for hikers and walkers taking to the hills. Their accuracy is a vital aid for many visitors to Scotland because unlike the rest of the UK, Scotland has very few public footpaths. Instead most of the land is 'open access', which means that it, *'sets out a right of responsible non-motorised access for recreational and other purposes, to land and inland water throughout Scotland, with a few exceptions...'* to quote from the Scottish Outdoor Access Code, all of which makes getting lost easy without a good map because there are few set paths.

Duart has some charts and surveys of the Castle on display that were prepared in the early days of the Ordinance Survey when it was known as the Board of Ordinance (BO). Following the defeat of the last Jacobite rebellion at Culloden in 1746 the BO mapped the Highlands to help the English navigate it and quell any further insurrection. Until then, maps often lacked the detail or accuracy necessary to manoeuvre troops and fight military campaigns.

Some of the sketches and paintings done by Paul Sandby, a military map maker and draftsman for the early surveys, are still used by the architects today when planning the restoration work.

The BO went on to survey and map the south coast of England, fearing the French Revolution might spread over the channel, and gradually set the standard for accurate map making in the UK and around the world.

The name Ordinance Survey was first printed on the *'Ordnance Survey of the Isle of Wight and part of Hampshire'* map of 1810.

In 1935 they began a 'retriangulation of Great Britain' and thousands of Trig Pillars were built as triangulation points. There is one to the south of Duart on the highest point between the Castle and Blacks Tower. One for the more energetic is close to Mull's second highest peak, the 776 metre Dùn da Ghaoithe, which can be seen from the castle on a clear day.

36 – ANDREW MACLEAN

'…He was very happy to fly me into the airfield at Glenforsa on Mull.'

As an introduction I should explain who I am. My name is Andrew Maclean and I have the great pleasure of being the youngest child of Sir Lachlan Maclean. As a result of this I have spent many of my summer holidays at Duart. I used to go there when my Grandfather, Lord Maclean, was still living there. I am also not employed by Duart, as I am part of the family and have a job in Edinburgh. This said, I have worked at the castle in the past as a holiday job.

I have also had the great pleasure to see the amount of work that goes on behind the scenes to get the castle up and ready for you all to enjoy. It is a lot more than just taking off a few dust sheets. Cabinets need to be refilled, silver polished, carpets hoovered, wood polished and I am sure I have missed a lot of other little jobs that take time.

2020 as we all know was a bit of a strange year with the country going into lockdown. This resulted in me trying to get to Mull as my job in Edinburgh had closed, and I thought being stuck in my flat in the middle of a city was going to be boring and hard work to keep positive. Moving to the west of Scotland to the beautiful island of Mull and the countryside around there, felt to me a much more sensible and enjoyable idea.

The one issue I did have was how to get to the island before lockdown. A special thanks here must be given to my uncle; he is a pilot and has a small private plane and he was very happy to fly me into the airfield at Glenforsa on Mull. Quite special as it only took about 30 minutes whereas diving from Edinburgh takes at least 3 hours then a 45-minute ferry trip.

After a bit of self-isolation, life at Duart began to take shape. Sir Lachlan (Dad) had decided that we should try and keep busy with jobs to keep the castle and grounds looking tidy and stop our minds from going to mush. This involved two Cobra meetings a week on Tuesday and Thursday mornings. In these meetings there was discussion of what was needed to be done and who would do what.

We had Anne doing gift shop sales online, Fiona doing tearoom organisation and planning plus a lot of signage, filming and editing for our social media films, Alison trying to keep my Dad up to date on his paperwork, which is easier said than done, and Ray doing everything else from hosting our Media films and helping with the editing and posting of the films, writing our risk assessment, and trying to make a 14th century Castle fit for social distancing. Not an easy job as one of the first issues are the narrow spiral stairs.

To keep our morale up we also had two evenings every week where we had a more relaxed time. On Fridays we had cake and wine and just chatted about nothing of any great relevance, it was just a nice unwind. On Sunday evenings we had supper together which was a lot of fun and a special note I think must been given to Anne as the puddings she produced were quite incredible. We also had some games after supper to keep us from getting too depressed. We had a few games of Uno and Jenga which was a lot of fun.

My jobs were mainly set outside and were not what I would call skilled. I did a bit of painting, weather proofing the gates to the gardens and the garage doors and the wood by the cattle grid at the entrance to the carpark. Dad and I also did a lot of bramble clearing around the grounds but made the most noticeable difference in the Millennium wood, which though I say it myself now looks amazing. Also, I collected seaweed from the beach for Carol to use in the garden.

As the summer rolled on and the restrictions were relaxed, we were able think about what sections of the business we could open. We started with just the grounds which first involved Jamie, the shepherd rounding up his sheep and trying to keep them from returning to the grounds around the castle; they seemed to be very partial to Alison's flowers. With the removal of the sheep, we then realized how much grass they eat. It was quite a job to keep the grass down to a manageable level, but I soon found the ride on mower and spent many happy hours driving around the grounds until the time came to return to Edinburgh as lockdown restrictions eased.

37 – DECEMBER 2020

The UK Government reveal that the first vaccines have been authorised for use in the UK, and the Scottish Government declares plans to start a COVID-19 vaccination programme. The First Minister announces that the easing of restrictions around Christmas will be limited to Christmas Day itself. From Boxing Day, all of Scotland will have Level 4 restrictions applied, including the closure of non-essential retail and hospitality. Travel between Scotland and the rest of the UK will not be legal from midnight on Sunday 20 December, except for a few specific exemptions. Scotland will go into lockdown from 5 January 2021 with a new legal requirement forbidding anyone from leaving their home except for essential purposes.

We said goodbye to Fiona and tears flowed. It was a melancholy, subdued time and the emerging news of a pending lockdown and tighter restrictions around Christmas and Hogmanay did nothing to lift our spirits. It was becoming serious again.

The days of visitors to the castle, and of being able to pop on a ferry and see family and friends seemed a long way off. The dark evenings and damp chilly air brought gloom and pessimism with them. We felt a long, lonely winter was ahead of us.

Then fate provided us a brief window to escape, for a short while.

It started with a death. The passing of Alison's 96-year-old great aunt who had led an extraordinary and inspirational life, one that deserves a book of its own. But that is for another time.

It was decreed that attending her funeral would not only be an opportunity to say farewell to a much-loved member of the family but would also give us an opportunity to wave at a few relatives from a safe distance, and with a fair wind see our children outside in something approaching their natural habitat to exchange Christmas gifts. All in all, a journey of a few yards over 500 miles each way.

With tentative arrangements in place, we discovered our car was overdue its Covid delayed MOT[9], so that was our first task, and as it happened, challenge.

Firstly, we discovered that leaving me in charge of the ferry booking was clearly a mistake as I had somehow booked our ferry crossings in reverse, so according to the tickets we were due to depart Oban just as we would be getting up. Problem averted thanks to a panicked phone call and considerable forbearance on the part of CalMac's customer service, we set sail later than anticipated but at least in the correct direction.

Then the car failed its MOT, on the not unreasonable grounds that three of its four wheels

---

[9] An MOT test is an annual check to ensure that your vehicle meets road safety and environmental standards.

were modelling tyres almost as bald as my head. The next challenge was to find replacements in time for our scheduled trip, and of course take the car back to the garage so that they could confirm the tyres were replaced and issue us with a new MOT certificate.

The nearest tyres we could find were in Fort William, so the following Monday off we sped over rain slick roads on tyres with the adhesive properties of greased kippers. It was the kind of day when the tops of the mountains disappeared into cloud and waterfalls cut ribbons of silver through the shimmering hillsides. It was delightfully picturesque and quintessentially Highland scenery.

Around halfway through our journey Alison, who was driving at the time, let out a squeal of alarm and announced that there was a police car chasing us. This proved to be true, its blue lights were flashing, and it was clearly indicating for us to pull over.

'What shall I do?'

I assumed her question was rhetorical. That or she was seriously considering gunning the engine and leading us on a high-speed chase until we finally ended up plummeting, Thelma and Louise style, into Loch Linnhe. A course of action that seemed unwise on bare tyres, and anyway we were in an economy Citroen and the pursuing forces of law and order were in a menacing silver BMW.

So, we pulled over and a representative of Argyll's law enforcement community, all of about 12 years old and apparently wearing a novelty beard he'd won in the station's Christmas raffle, bent down and asked Alison if she knew why he stopped us?

I am of the generation when I expect a police constable to doff his helmet, bend at the knees and greet me with a courteous 'Good day sir.' And preferably be old enough not to have to climb onto a stool before bopping a miscreant on the head with his truncheon, so I was about to ask him if his parents knew he wasn't in school when fate intervened.

A lorry sped past and deposited most of a large puddle over our adolescent inquisitor. Alison thanked him for protecting us and suggested he come around to the passenger side, which he did, shaking himself like a dog that had just enjoyed a swim.

Anyway, it turned out they knew we were without an MOT, but fortunately we could show proof that we'd had a test and were on our way to a pre-booked appointment to have the tyres replaced. This satisfied our soggy cherub who bade us farewell in a kindly fashion and returned to his car, where his chum helped him up into his booster seat, and we went our separate ways.

Drama over we pootled to Fort William, tyres were changed and we headed back to Oban for the MOT re-sit, and as the sun drained from the sky, we finally got on the road south.

We had booked a night in Glasgow and pulled into a budget chain hotel to be greeted by a formidable receptionist who demanded to know why we were travelling.

'Just passing through…,' I said.

Which was as true as it was succinct.

'You do know that in Scotland it's illegal to travel unless it is for work?' She said.

'But you took our booking without asking us why' was all I could think of to say. Again, feeling that brevity and honesty were my friends.

'You do know that in Scotland it's illegal to travel unless it is for work?'

'But you took our booking without asking us why'.

'You do know that in Scotland it's illegal to travel unless it is for work?'

'But…'

Alison decided the time was ripe for logical intervention. 'We're on our way to a funeral' she said.

'That's good enough for me, here's your key, you'll be in room 26.'

'But you took our booking…' I said in a petulant tone as I was ushered away.

The following morning was bright and cheerful. We were on the road in good time and as we crossed the border into England, we agreed that all the hassles of yesterday were behind us and, aside from the sadness of the funeral, it would be a fine trip.

'What else could possibly go wrong?' I said tuning the radio to a news channel.

'With the NHS weeks from being overwhelmed, and a higher death toll than the first wave predicted without new restrictions, the Prime Minister, Chief Medical Officer, Chief Scientific Advisor, and Cabinet agreed there was no alternative to tougher national measures…'

And that is how we came to spend a week living in a hotel room in Cambridge. We cancelled visits to friends and family, went for government mandated exercise, went to the funeral where we mingled at an awkward distance, had a takeaway meal just for the novelty of being able to have it delivered, and returned home to Mull early, with Christmas presents undistributed and our nearest and dearest unhugged.

We arrived back at a damp Duart. Misty rain was clinging to the mountains, obscuring the views and muting sounds. Even the sheep seemed listless and tired. Walking around the castle it seemed forlorn and dank. Dust sheets covering displays made ominous shapes and cast strange shadows in the dim half-light.

It is a fact of castle life that it is often cold and damp out of season. There is a reason why Mull isn't a winter destination for the masses. My daily 'round' involves emptying several dehumidifiers and they always seem to have collected plenty of moisture from the atmosphere.

Water penetration has been a constant problem in the exhibition room fireplaces which are directly above the large fireplace in the Banqueting Hall two floors below. The walls are thinner because of the chimney flues. So, I got to light a fire in the hall twice a week to help warm it through and dry the walls out a bit. Once lit, I could not leave it because of the possibility of spitting embers doing damage. Although it's probable that the castle is too damp to burn, the exhibits are most certainly not.

Thus, a lot of this book was written with my back to a raging fire. Open fires are deceptive. They look warm but only heat a radius of a metre or so into the room. I would sit at the big table with the back of my coat melting and frost forming down the front.

Bezhad took to greeting me like the master of the house and bowed deeply when he walked in. I could get used to this, I thought to myself, savouring my coffee like a fine port and leaning back on my chair to better survey 'my' great hall.

30 seconds later I was picking myself up from the floor, where I had narrowly avoided tipping myself backwards into the fireplace. I mopped up my coffee and thought perhaps lairdship was not for me after all.

Although the shop was closed the on-line store continued, and much to everyone's delight Anne's hard work was paying off and internet sales were booming. We had expected the trajectory to fall away after we closed but sales were refreshingly healthy.

As Christmas approached, Andy went home for the holiday season, Anne left the caravan, which is not designed for the full force of a Scottish winter and moved into temporary bricks and mortar lodging in Craignure. Just the Chief, Alison, Behzad and me remained onsite as Christmas week started.

Christmas can be a difficult time. People in the UK were advised, then instructed, to minimise travel and gatherings and only to meet on Christmas Day itself. Another almost total lockdown would commence from Boxing Day.

The Chief popped over to family on the mainland for Christmas, so he was away for a couple of nights and due to return on Boxing Day. On Christmas morning we had Zoom meetings with family and exchanged Christmas greetings then Anne came to us for the rest of the day.

An enormous dinner was consumed, we chatted and generally took each other's minds off family and friends, Bezhad joined us in the evening and a merry old time was had by all.

We knew that we were fortunate. We might be missing the company of our nearest and dearest, but many people's lives had been permanently changed because of the pandemic.

There were empty seats at festive tables around the world. People in hospitals were fighting for their lives, carers and medical staff were working ridiculously long shifts, frequently in grim conditions, elderly people in nursing homes, often frail and confused, were missing precious moments with grandchildren on Christmas Day.

This had been a tough year for many people and the poignancy and nostalgia associated with Christmas must have been unbearable for a lot of people.

At Duart we tried not to take our relatively good fortune for granted. We had lived through a season like no other.

December 2020

Dry days 2,
Max temperature 12.5,
Min temperature -2.5,
Max wind speed 46.8 mph,
Monthly rainfall 12.98 mm.

38 – HOW FAR?

There are plenty of settlements named for Macleans around the world. Discounting Maclean Counties and Districts in the USA and setting aside landmarks, streets, schools and colleges, there is still an impressive list that stretches around the world from Canada and the USA to the Bahamas, Australia and Africa.

Maybe the most 'Maclean' town is the Australian settlement of, you guessed it, **Maclean**, in the state of New South Wales. It was named after Alexander Grant McLean, who had been made New South Wales Surveyor-General in November 1861. It's often cited as Australia's most Scottish town, hosting Highland Games, a Maclean Highland Gathering and it is home to the Bicentennial Scottish Cairn, made from rocks from Australia and Scotland. It is approximately 16,606.33km (10,318.70 miles) away from Duart Castle.

Then again, maybe one or more of the following could claim the title?

Mcleans Ridges, NSW Australia,
16,543km - 10,280 miles
Maclean, Queensland, Australia,
16,426km - 10,207miles
Macleantown, Buffalo City, South Africa,
10,514km - 6,533miles
McLean's Town, Grand Bahama Island, Caribbean,
6,381km - 3,965 miles
McLean, Virginia, USA,
5,296km - 3,291 miles
Mcleansville, North Carolina, USA
5,675km - 3,526 miles
Mcleansboro, Illinois, USA
6,035km - 3,750 miles
Mclean, Texas, USA,
5,296km - 3,291 miles
McLean, Illinois, USA
5,856km - 3,639 miles
McLean, Ohio, USA,
5,616km - 3,490 miles
McLean, Nebraska USA,
6,181km - 3,840 miles
McLean, Saskatchewan, Canada,
5,850km - 3,635 miles
Maclean, Malawi, Africa,
8,459km - 5,256 miles

There are probably more that I have included, so do let me know of any omissions.

All distances are a straight line, rounded and taken from Craignure ferry port. They are approximate, so if you decide to walk to Duart from, for example, Maclean, Texas, do not blame me if it's a few miles more than I've said.

39 - FALLOUT

*'If all the economists were laid end to end,
they would not reach a conclusion.'*[10]

In this chapter I will be looking at the economic impact of the pandemic during 2020 and take a brief peak at what 2021 and beyond may hold. It is quite hard to write a cheerful account of a global crisis as it is, and economists and financial journalists are not generally noted for their cheerful public persona. I guess if you are an economic expert you want to appear trustworthy, calm and analytical, perhaps a tad on the boring side even.

Alison and I are both products of accountant fathers. My late father had a keen sense of humour and Alison's is a charming and jovial old sausage. However, there is an accountant gene that they share, a disposition that favours orderliness and an appreciation of things being 'just so'. Numbers are either right or wrong, and accountants, in our

---

[10] Widely attributed to George Bernard Shaw.

experience, share that approach to life.

Alison and I have not inherited the accountancy gene. A fact that the Chief occasionally exploits for humours effect, especially when Alison describes the difference between two figures as 'quite a lot' or 'probably not much' rather than with the military precision of a bookkeeping personality. Likewise, I have ordered startling quantities of lightbulbs for the castle, enough to illuminate Las Vegas, because I did not let small details like decimal points intrude upon my paperwork. Fortunately, the nice lady at our suppliers was kind enough to query my order.

'This must happen a lot' I said to her.

'No, not really...'

Before we plunge onwards, to avoid all that tedious referencing business I have listed my primary sources at the end of this chapter. In my experience, this also works better with Kindle and e-readers. I will also take this opportunity to remind you that you may disagree with the resources I've used, their findings and even with the whole pandemic. That's cool and dandy. I am sure that some of the figures are open to debate. Indeed, they should be, challenge and refinement are bedrocks of science.

I am not taking a political stance either. My aim is simply to give a flavour of the impact of an unprecedented year. I will, eventually, work my way back to Duart Castle, but as The Beatles once sung, *'It's a long and winding road...'*

So, dim the lights, pour yourself a cocktail, stick an umbrella in it, put some soft music on in the background, loosen your collar and sit back – we are going to stroke the naked thighs of data and fondle some statistics in the sexy world of economics.

After facing one of the most testing environments in history, the worldwide economy is predicted to start clawing its way out of decline during 2021. One market analysist described it as a swoosh shaped graph, sudden drop, and gradual climb back up. Think logo of a certain sportswear brand, go on, just do it!

In a statement published in October 2020 the World Health Organisation stated:

'The COVID-19 pandemic has led to a dramatic loss of human life worldwide and presents an unprecedented challenge to public health, food systems and the world of work. The economic and social disruption caused by the pandemic is devastating; tens of millions of people are at risk of falling into extreme poverty, while the number of undernourished people, currently estimated at nearly 690 million, could increase by up to 132 million by the end of the year.'

Globally millions of businesses and the people that rely upon them are at risk. Some estimates put the figure at close to half of the world's workforce will have their livelihoods threatened. The effects of the pandemic reach more than just employment. Border closures, trade restrictions and lockdowns have impacted international food supply chains and caused unprecedented government, business and personal borrowing.

In 2020 the contraction in the UK economy *'was more than twice as much as the previous largest annual fall on record...'* according to the Office of National Statistics.

A UK House of Commons Briefing published in

January 2021 stated:

'The magnitude of the recession caused by the coronavirus outbreak is unprecedented in modern times. UK GDP[11] was 25% lower during the depth of the crisis in April 2020 than it was only two months earlier in February.'

It goes on to point out that a fall in GDP in the first quarter of 2021 was likely too, but that the vaccine roll-out was expected to herald a gradual improvement.

The UK Government's budget deficit (the difference between its spending and revenues) is projected to reach a peace time record in 2020/21.

The UK Government support to businesses, workers and household incomes is likely to have cost around £280 billion in 2020. The longer the crisis continues, the more the cost to government will rise. Its debt is increasing as the Government borrows more to fund spending.

One area that has been relativity resistant to the pandemic in the UK is unemployment. Although there has been an increase in the number of people seeking work, the job retention (furloughing) schemes have kept people off the unemployment figures. When the scheme finishes it's not known how many of the businesses they've been furloughed from will continue. It seems likely that some, especially in retail and hospitality, will struggle to re-establish themselves.

In December 2020, a report published jointly by

---

[11] Gross Domestic Product - the total value of goods produced and services provided in a country during one year.

the Scottish Government and the Convention of Scottish Local Authorities (COSLA) concluded that '...*the pandemic is impacting disproportionately on people in poverty, low-paid workers, children and young people, older people, disabled people, minority ethnic groups and women. Lower earners have seen steeper falls in income because of the pandemic and a range of evidence suggests income inequalities are widening and isolation and loneliness have increased*'.

On a more positive note, the report also found that, '...*there is also evidence of positive impacts on community cohesion and empowerment, the pandemic is speeding up the adoption of digital technologies, with the potential to improve business profitability and access to services such as healthcare and the rise in home working could spread well-paid jobs more evenly across the country*'.

Looking forward, VisitBritain estimates that 2021 should show an improvement from 2020. For visitor numbers from abroad there are variations between slightly higher numbers of European visitors and significantly lower for long haul travellers. Taken together it still amounts to only 25% of 2019 levels overall. As I write this in March 2021 new outbreaks in parts of Europe and the rise of the Delta Variant may set these estimates back.

Long haul travel will be affected more than local. Some sources say it will not be before 2023 that long distance tourism is at anything like 2019 levels. In 2020 we really missed the visitors from abroad. Due to the scattering of Macleans around the world during the last few centuries we always welcome a lot of Clan guests from far away.

In 2019 Macleans signing the guest book included

over 300 from the USA, more than 80 from Canada, 80 from Australia and nearly 25 from New Zealand. In 2020 we had 5 from Australia and just 1 each from the USA, Canada and New Zealand. All of those I spoke to were already in the UK for work or study when lockdown begun.

Locally, the domestic tourism market is forecast to recover to £61.7bn in domestic tourism spending in 2021; this is up 79% compared to 2020 but still only 67% of the level of spending seen in 2019.

VisitBritain point out that in their forecasts... *'As with our inbound forecast, this is a short-term forecast that describes one possible outturn and involves many assumptions and simplifications due to the fast-moving and uncertain situation.'*

On March 3rd 2021, the following figures were released as part of the UK governments budget statement:

- UK economy forecast to return to pre-Covid levels by middle of 2022.
- Annual growth set to rebound by 4% in 2021, followed by 7.3% growth in 2022.
- Unemployment expected to peak at 6.5% in 2022, lower than 11.9% previously predicted.
- UK to borrow a peacetime record of £355bn in 2021.
- Borrowing to total £234bn in 2021-22.
- Debt as a share of GDP to fall from 4.5% in 2021 to 3.5% in 2022-23.

The bottom line is, we are going to see an increasing number of domestic and overseas visitors, but it has been predicted to be at least two years before we start to see numbers returning to pre-pandemic levels. In the meantime, it'll be hard going. As it will be for businesses and people everywhere.

All this assumes the vaccine programme works and we do not fall prey to a second pandemic, a mutant variation, or invasion from Mars.

It doesn't take a world class economist with a crystal ball or two to tell you that in the immediate aftermath of the pandemic the financial outlook for most economies will be similar to the UKs at best, and for some it could be catastrophic.

There are huge debts to be paid, for government borrowing, for furloughed staff, for vaccines, increased use of health services and for kick-starting faltering economies.

Which all boils down to less disposable income in our pockets and greater, and arguably more pressing demands upon Government spending than historic buildings, like Duart for example.

One can make a good case for protecting heritage sites and investing in the story of our nation, and of the Clan Maclean. The cultural legacy we leave for future generations should be rich and rewarding, with an appreciation for the preservation of our history. Nevertheless, it would be understandable if restoration projects were not at the front of the queue when it comes to state grants in the next few years.

Gloomy stuff indeed.

So, let us end this chapter on a positive.

You.

You are an adorable specimen who should rightly

be lauded as an example to everyone else for your delightful personality and gorgeous smile.

As if that wasn't enough, you have contributed a little bit of your hard-earned cash towards restoring one of Scotland's treasures - Duart Castle - by purchasing this book.

Thank you.

If you would like to know more about the castle restoration project you can find information at www.maclean.org/duart-appeal

———

Primary sources:

- who.int/news/item/13-10-2020-impact-of-covid-19-on-people's-livelihoods-their-health-and-our-food-systems
- nationalperformance.gov.scot/scotlands-wellbeing-impact-covid-19
- commonslibrary.parliament.uk/research-briefings/cbp-8866/
- www.imperial.ac.uk/mrc-global-infectious-disease-analysis/covid-19/report-12-global-impact-covid-19/
- Visitbritain.org
- Office for National Statistics (UK)

40 - VIRTUE MINE HONOUR

It had been a wonderful, beguiling, and difficult year. A period of light and shade unprecedented in recent times. For some it brought chaos, fear and panic, hardship and loneliness, loss and grief.

To many it also provided relief, community spirit and hope. Carers, key workers of types too numerous to list here, small acts of kindness and a huge mobilisation of resources.

Mistakes were made, errors and omissions at national and local level. Policies and responses written 'on the fly', science challenged, and conspiracy theories hatched.

Duart simply continued. 'If only the walls could speak' is a phrase we often hear when visitors are wandering along its corridors. If they could, they would probably acknowledge it as just another chapter in its long, illustrious, and sometimes bloody, history.

The Castle weathered the winter in its traditional, slightly leaky way. The Sea Room had a complete overhaul, as has our small staff office. New paving has been laid around the courtyard and outside, most of the scaffolding has moved from the Sound of Mull side of the castle and is now over-looking the car park as the wall gets a thorough repointing.

The work carries on regardless.

Sir Lachlan Maclean, Fiona, Anne, Arianna, Alison, Andy, Jonny, Behzad, Carol, Andrew Maclean and I are just a small part of its story. We just happened to be around during one of the many times it has faced a challenge head on.

On the 5 March 2021 we waved goodbye to Anne. She had decided to move back to New Zealand to be closer to her family.

Fiona opted not to return for the 2021 season.

As I write this in March 2021 Andrew Maclean is back at work.

Andy and Behzad are both beavering away diligently. Jonny is still restoring windows and pops over occasionally to swap them around.

Arianna and her husband moved to the mainland as the 2020 season closed. On the 1st June 2021 she gave birth to their first child, Lance Pretorious.

Carol comes in to perform those rituals that gardeners enjoy. Sowing seeds, weeding, collecting seaweed and generally keeping the tearoom supplied with fresh produce.

Alison and I are still here. Winter has been quiet but productive. We have done some decorating in the cottage and various projects around the castle and grounds. We have just enjoyed being on Mull really.

The Chief has been busy. He's soldiered on and sorted out all manner of old paperwork and archives, kept spirits up with Thursday night drinks loosely disguised as business meetings and sorted out staffing for the year ahead.

On 9 May 2021 we opened the castle for the 2021 season. Only for five days a week but after a slow start business is steadily building.

There's a story about an old man with his broom sweeping leaves. He tells his young apprentice that it is the very same broom he started out with over 60 years ago, when he was an apprentice himself.

'Of course, I've changed the handle a few times…and I change the brush every year…but it's still the same broom.'

Duart is like that broom. It's been built, rebuilt, altered, ruined, renovated and restored countless times. But it is still Duart. Still standing guard over the Sound of Mull because, like the old man's broom, whatever happens it is loved and looked after, used and appreciated.

It welcomes visitors and friends from around the world, Macleans, Rankins and many others step through its doors. The weather may not always be sunny, but the welcome is always warm and heartfelt. Wherever you have travelled from, whatever your story, when you get to Duart you are stepping into history.

For Duart Castle it was just another year in its rich and varied history.

For most of us 2020 was a year like no other.

41 – WHAT A YEAR THAT WAS

A lonely year for visitor contact, but a great year to build friendships within our bubble and to test my ability to adapt and thrive.
Anne

Joy in growing food, companionship in those around me but a new appreciation of solitude and comfort in peace.
Alison

So long mad pyjama lady and thank you for the nice lavender.
Shauna the sheep.

Every morning that I am here I look up at the castle and think, wow!
Behzad

Experiencing 2020 was relentless, unforgiving, but also a positive intervention, a chance to learn skills and reach a new potential.
Fiona

I certainly remember a lot of laughter.
Andrew Maclean

You can make a difficult situation easier for yourself if you stick to the plan, keeping these words in mind, as a short summary of 2020 - Resolution, passion, commitment.
Jonny

I will remember 2020 not just as the year of coronavirus and lockdowns, but as the year I worked my last season at Duart Castle. I have now moved back to the mainland after 4 amazing years living and working on the wonderful Isle of Mull.
Arianna

Companionship, joy in the simple pleasures of a simple life, fortified by the amazing spirit of resilience and comradery on Mull and in communities around the world.
Ray

Better than 2018 not as good as 1996 but with cleaner hands.
Andy

My highlight of 2020. I was married at Duart Castle to my long term partner. A truly happy day with many plants eaten and drunk!
Carol

I knew we wouldn't fail in lockdown as we had special people in our bubble who helped see us through.
The Chief

ABOUT THE AUTHOR

Writing and self-publishing isn't a lucrative career. Even though I have five books 'under my belt' I'm still waiting to be catapulted into another tax bracket. When I added the total of my book income to my last tax return, I was given a rebate!

I write because I love doing it. The deal I made with the Chief was that in return for the income generated from this tome going towards the restoration of the castle, I could promote my other works. Being a writer suits an introvert like me – whereas publicity does not, so 'blowing my own trumpet' isn't a comfortable feeling.

Then again, if I can sell a few of my other books I might get an even bigger rebate on my next tax return. If you are tempted, they are all as cheap as I can make them on Amazon.

I'll finish this small introduction by saying, *'Downwardly Mobile'* and *'Still Following Rainbows'* are not dissimilar to Duart Castle in Lockdown in style and humour. *'Even Unicorns Die'* is not for the faint of heart – it's quite sweary and dark. *'The Mitchley Waltz'* is completely different – it's a love story that's very close to my heart.

Now, here comes the self-aggrandising puff, including some nice reviews that good natured people have written about my books, so you don't just have to take my word for it.

———

Born in London and raised in Hertfordshire and Suffolk, Ray was drifting through high school until he discovered punk rock. From then on, he spent his time nurturing his lack of musical ability, until realising too late that exam success might have been a better option. Despite his abysmal school exam results, he went on to forge a career as a nurse, such was the desperation of the NHS in the early 80s.

After a second career in Social Housing and Community Development he and Alison left the rat race, swapped their house for a motorhome and took to the open road.

Life on the road re-ignited a desire to write that had never been entirely extinguished despite the best efforts of his teachers. His previous writing experience includes company annual reports, a punk rock fanzine and forging notes from his mother to excuse him from PE.

In 2018 he published his first book, Downwardly Mobile, documenting his and Alison's escape from the rat race and spending the best part of 2016 on the road, working at festivals and discovering the UK from the vantage point of a Motorhome called Mavis.

'You could imagine yourself looking out of the window and seeing it with your own eyes, such was the way it was described. Be prepared to laugh out loud, I got some funny looks when reading this on the bus when I would chuckle and then cry in equal measure. Be sure to read this book.'

After moving to the Isle of Mull and living in their motorhome while working at a certain castle, Ray published the next instalment of his and Alison's adventures in Still Following Rainbows.

It documents the highs and lows of adjusting to life and work on Mull. With snippets of history and vivid descriptions of the landscape you'll feel like you're along for the ride, and with Ray's insightful observations of people, places and situations this book will produce tears and explosions of laughter in equal measure.

"I cannot recommend this book highly enough. Ray is a gifted storyteller, and his words have the power to draw out a whole range of emotions as we journey with himself, Alison, and Mavis to a new life on a Scottish island. It's real, it's raw and it will make you want to visit Mull!"

At the beginning of the lockdown in 2020 Ray decided to do his bit for the Covid-19 lock-down and raid his scrap book for unpublished articles, short stories and pieces cut from his other books as an economy-priced diversion for everyone stuck at home. So, he published Even Unicorns Die - a collection of short stories, articles and assorted nonsense.

"Wow! This is very different from Ray's autobiographical writing: be warned! It's a delight to read - but don't let that fool you into expectations of a collection of lightweight, heart-warming, feel-good fuzz. This writing has depth and darkness. There are political observations, stories with unexpected stings, thought-provoking reflections, hellish humour, and an alphabet rhyme which you wouldn't want anywhere near your children! It's good. Very good! Order a copy at once!"

Rays writing in 2020 went from the ridiculous to

the sublime with the publication of The Mitchley Waltz.

London 1955 – 1958

As the country was finally recovering from war, one woman in North London received a grim diagnosis. She recorded the events that changed her life in her diaries.

Trying to make the best of her confinement in hospital, Iris had to face the fear that her blossoming career as a ballroom dancing instructor may now be over, along with any possibility of finding love with any of her potential suitors.

As the years passed, the diaries recorded her personal traumas and anxieties, her dreams and ambitions and they revealed a survivor who faced her worries with a steely determination and fought to overcome the legacy of permanent frailty.

Ignoring medical advice and returning to the dancefloor, could she ever make her dreams a reality, and could she risk opening her heart to the shy widower who had started attending her classes?

After her death in 2018, her son found her diaries among her possessions and set about transcribing them. Along with additional research and commentary he has brought the London that Iris knew in the 1950s back to life in vivid Technicolour.

"It's an excellent time capsule of life around that time, made all the more poignant by the true story of one woman's trials and brought to life with the author's scene setting and accompanying footnotes."

Thank you. Stay safe.

Ray
June 2021

Printed in Great Britain
by Amazon